THE COMPLETE ASIAN REPORT WRITER

GRAHAM COLIN-JONES

TIMES BOOKS INTERNATIONAL
Singapore • Kuala Lumpur

Edited by Pang Guek Cheng

© 1989 Times Editions Pte Ltd

Published by Times Books International
an imprint of Times Editions Pte Ltd
Times Centre, 1 New Industrial Road
Singapore 1953

2nd Floor, Wisma Hong Leong Yamaha
50 Jalan Penchala
46050 Petaling Jaya
Selangor Darul Ehsan
Malaysia

Reprinted 1992

All rights reserved. No part of this publication may be reproduced, stored in a retrieval system or transmitted, in any form or by any means, electronic, mechanical, photocopying, recording or otherwise, without the prior permission of the copyright owner.

Printed by Jin Jin Printing Industry Pte Ltd

ISBN 981 204 310 1

Contents

Preface *v*
Acknowledgements *vi*
The author *vii*

1 What is a report? *1*

Definition *1*
Functions *2*
Importance *4*
Qualities *4*
Types *5*

2 Before you start *11*

Terms of reference *11*
Purpose *12*
Know the reader *16*

3 Getting the facts *18*

Sources of information *20*
Interviews *22*
Questionnaires *25*

4 Planning the report *38*

Selecting your information *40*
Organising the information *44*

5 Writing the introduction *58*

6 Using language that communicates *70*

Correct *70*
Concise *74*
Clear *78*
Cohesive *88*
Objective *94*
Readable *95*
Appropriate *97*

7 Making a visual impact *101*

Layout *102*
Illustrations *104*

8 Writing the conclusion *122*

Where to put it *124*
How to write it *126*

9 Writing the recommendations *130*

What is a suitable recommendation? *131*
Do all reports require one? *131*
How to write it *132*
What language to use *133*
The problem of punctuation *133*

10 Revising your report *140*

Read it again *140*
Use a checklist *141*
Ask a colleague *148*

11 Applying the finishing touches *150*

Synopsis *150*
Title page *153*
Table of contents *157*

Bibliography *160*
Letter of transmittal *161*

12 Sample reports *165*

First report *165*
Second report *173*

Appendices *186*
Bibliography *204*
Index *206*

Preface

Report writing is generally considered to be a tedious, time-consuming task which all professionals have to endure from time to time, without necessarily reaching a level of competence that meets with their own approval, let alone that of their boss. This need not be the case.

This book is designed to lead all report writers, regardless of nationality, through the steps necessary to ensure that a report is thoroughly researched, logically planned, clearly written and presented in such a way as to create the maximum impact on the reader.

The book is, however, directed in particular at those who are required to write reports in English, even though English is not their native language. Consequently, there is special emphasis on the use of English in writing the introduction, the body, the conclusion and the recommendations section of reports.

Since the book is intended for self-study, the explanations and advice are written in clear, easy-to-read English so that all potential and actual report writers can understand. These explanations are enhanced by authentic examples drawn from reports written by Asians who have experience and skill in the writing of reports. Thus the reader is provided with ample guidance on the most efficient and effective approach to report writing.

Report writing may never become an enjoyable task, but, if the suggestions in this book are followed, it can become interesting, challenging, and above all profitable in terms of time saved and end-product quality.

Acknowledgements

I should like to express my thanks to the following who have provided me with invaluable assistance:

> Mr Tony Chan, Ms Yeoh Hsin Ling, Mr Garry Prior, who permitted me to make use of reports they had written.
> Robyn Blood and Riza Apolonio who typed the manuscript so quickly and efficiently.
> As always, my wife Yvonne for her help and support.

Thanks also to the following who have allowed me to reproduce extracts/illustrations from their reports:

> Robert E. Burgen, US Department of Agriculture Forest Service; IAEA Bulletin; Journal of Forestry; Ministry of Finance, Singapore; National Productivity Board, Singapore; David L. Rumpf, Department of Industrial Engineering, Northeastern University; and Trans Island Bus Services Ltd.

The Author

Graham Colin-Jones is the English language training specialist at the Asian Development Bank in Manila, Philippines. He is responsible for designing programmes which will help non-native speakers of English to improve both their written and oral communication. In addition, he conducts seminars on a variety of topics, including Writing Correct English and Report and Memo Writing.

Since graduating from the University of Lancaster in 1973 with a BA (Hons), he has obtained three postgraduate teaching qualifications, including an MA in Teaching English as a Foreign Language, in which his main area of study was self-access language learning.

He is also the author of *All About Words* and *The Complete Asian Letter Writer*. Both these are self-study handbooks based on his expertise in self-access language learning and 14 years of teaching/training experience in England, Hong Kong, Singapore and the Philippines. He was also the language columnist for a Singapore newspaper, and gave a series of radio talks on the use of English.

His knowledge, skill and experience are evident in this comprehensive yet easy-to-read book on report writing.

*To my children
Antonia and Alastair*

1 What is a report?

When students are informed that they are going to learn how to write reports or when an employee is asked by his superior for the first time to prepare a report, the reaction is generally a negative one. The former tend to groan at the prospect of learning a skill which they believe will be a tedious process, and will require hard work. The latter realises that, although he lacks experience in writing reports, he will be assessed by his superior on the basis of this report.

It is true that report writing requires hard work, but it can be interesting as you achieve a deeper knowledge of a particular subject or find a solution to a problem and so know you are making a valuable contribution to your company. Report writing need not be such a daunting prospect to the young employee provided he tackles the task in a systematic way and spends time organising his thoughts and the information he has collected.

The starting point for being able to write a report is knowing what a report is.

A DEFINITION

A very simple definition of a report is

a presentation of information.

The most common reports that immediately come to mind are school reports, weather reports and accident reports. School reports provide a written record of a student's performance which is to be presented to the student's parents. Weather reports may be presented orally but they still convey information. Accident reports can be completed at a police station providing information as to what happened, when and how.

In fact most companies have accident report forms which employees are required to complete when the need arises. Such reports require little preparation and the provision of a standardised form means that the writer does not have to worry too much about the layout.

In other words, the above types of report cause few problems to the writer. It is the longer written report requiring considerable thought and preparation that needs guidance and practice. Such a report can be defined more precisely as

> **a document which gives information, reports findings, puts forward ideas and sometimes makes recommendations on a specific subject for a specific reader.**

FUNCTIONS

This definition of a report indicates three general functions of reports. These functions can be expressed more precisely:

1. **To give information**

    The information stated in a report can fulfil any one or more of the following functions:

    - to state the history or background of a particular project
    - to describe a process or an existing situation
    - to enable a record to be kept for future use

2. **To report findings**

    The findings include the information that you have obtained from your investigation and any experiments you may have conducted. Thus the report may need:

    - to provide details on the progress of a project

What is a report?

- to explain the reasons for accidents, delays, damage, etc.
- to state the results of any experiments, surveys etc.

3. **To put forward ideas**

   Any ideas that you put forward must, of course, be based on the information you have obtained. In other words, it is necessary to be able to analyse this information objectively in order to formulate sound ideas and logical conclusions. Such ideas and conclusions serve:

   - to evaluate a proposal, system or piece of equipment
   - to propose a solution to a problem
   - to recommend improvements and action to be taken

Example

In Hong Kong, the Mass Transit Railway (MTR) has been functioning for several years and in Singapore, the Mass Rapid Transit (MRT) has recently started running. However, before any decision could be taken on whether or not to have an underground system a report had to be written regarding the traffic situation at the time. This report would have had:

- to state any historical background that could have a bearing on an MTR/MRT decision, e.g. growth in car ownership.
- to describe the existing situation on the roads, e.g. traffic jams, particularly at certain places.
- to explain the reasons for increasing delays, e.g. more traffic, narrow roads.
- to compare and choose between alternatives, e.g. build an MTR/MRT, widen roads, improve the existing bus/tram services, restrict car ownership, increase charges for those driving in congested areas at peak times.
- to propose a solution/to recommend improvements.

The suggested alternatives would all lead to an improvement in the existing situation so the solution of constructing the MTR/MRT may not be the only alternative to be implemented.

IMPORTANCE

Even though the above example mentions only a few of the points that would be raised in a detailed report on the need for an MTR/MRT, this is sufficient to indicate the importance of reports.

Providing the report contains the necessary information, the reader of the report is able to make sound decisions. Good reports are therefore essential to management in order to save the latter time in obtaining information and to guide management in the decision-making process.

QUALITIES

Having said that management requires good reports, what are the qualities of a good report?

1. **Accuracy**

    The information given in the report must be accurate. In addition it needs to be up to date. Statistics for three years ago are not particularly useful when one can obtain last year's figures.

2. **Conciseness**

    Conciseness applies both to the content of the report, so that only relevant information is included, and to the language so that as few words as possible are used.

3. **Completeness**

    Although the report should be concise it must also be complete. Nothing relevant should be omitted.

4. **Clarity**

    The report must be clear to the specific reader in three areas:

    i) The **language** must be easy to understand.
    ii) There must be a **logical sequence** in the presentation of

What is a report?

        information so that the reader can follow the progression of ideas without any difficulty.

iii) The **layout** of the report must be neat and clear so that the reader can easily locate any specific piece of information.

TYPES OF REPORT

There are many different types of report, but the following classification will enable us to understand more clearly the function of some common types.

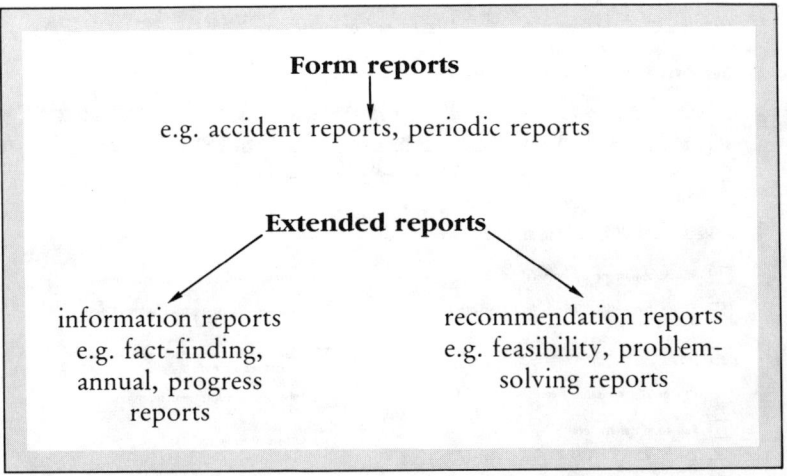

1. Form reports

Pre-printed forms are often provided by companies for the completion of reports which are frequently written. Since the structure of the report is supplied, an employee who has no experience of writing an extended report can be expected to complete a form in order to provide the necessary details concerning either an accident (see Fig. 1.1) or an incident (see Fig. 1.2) that has occurred at work. This is particularly important since it is likely to be the manual worker who is involved in accidents or incidents.

The Complete Asian Report Writer

WORK INJURY/ACCIDENT REPORT

1. PARTICULARS OF THE INJURED

   NAME: Ali bin Yusof AGE: 21
   ADDRESS: Blk 152, Ling Tuck Rd #03-152 NRIC NO: 0182-3567/C
   OCCUPATION: Machine operator DEPT/SECTION: Printing
   YEARS OF SERVICE: 2 yrs. EXPECTED PERIOD OF
   NATURE OF INJURY: _____ ABSENCE: _____
   (Inclusive of part of body injured)

2. PARTICULARS OF ACCIDENT/WORK INJURY

   DATE: 1.3.89 TIME: 2120 hrs PLACE OF ACCIDENT: Cosmos Printing

   DESCRIPTION OF ACCIDENT/WORK INJURY:

   As we were washing the printing machine, three fingers of his right hand got caught in the rollers. The operator in charge pressed the emergency button.

3. CAUSES OF ACCIDENT/WORK INJURY

   - [ ] Struck against or by objects
   - [ ] Struck by sliding, falling, flying or other moving objects
   - [x] Caught in or between objects
   - [ ] Fall or slip on same level
   - [ ] Fall to different level
   - [ ] Over exertion
   - [ ] Contact with temperature extremes
   - [ ] Exposure to or contact with electric current
   - [ ] Exposure to or contact with harmful substances or radiations
   - [ ] Inhalation, absorption, injestion, poisoning etc
   - [ ] Others (Please specify)

4. WHAT CAN BE DONE TO PREVENT A RECURRENCE?

   Operators must be alerted to this danger and made to be more careful

   DATE: 2.3.89 SIGNATURE OF INJURED: _____

   N.B. The purpose of the accident/work injury report is to find out the causes of the accident and to state what steps need to be taken to prevent the same type of accident/work injury from recurring.

Fig 1.1 Form for an accident report

What is a report?

```
To:   President/Marketing Mgr/F & A Mgr/Fire & Safety Officer

                    INTERNAL OCCURRENCE REPORT

1.   Reported by _____

2.   Date of Occurrence _____

3.   Nature of Occurrence (brief description)
     _____
     _____
     _____
     _____
     _____
     _____
     _____
     _____
     _____
     _____
     _____

4.   Any injury to personnel or damage to equipment/property
     _____
     _____

5.   Any delay in loading activities _____
     Any contamination of products? _____
     _____

6.   Immediate actions taken (if any) _____
     _____
     _____

              _____
                   SIGNATURE
Note:  This occurrence form must be completed and sent to the above
       persons within ONE day after the incident.
```

Fig 1.2 Form for internal occurrence report

Salesmen are required to provide regular reports on their sales performance, and so standardised forms will save them a lot of time and enable them to spend more time on selling and less on paperwork. In addition, the reader of form reports can pick out the information he wants more quickly since he is accustomed to the format of the form.

Form reports also encourage writers to be concise since there is insufficient space for long-winded writing.

2. Extended reports

Whereas form reports are restricted in length by the amount of space on the form, the extended report can be of any length depending on the amount of information that needs to be included. A so-called extended report may be only one or two pages long, in which case it may be given to the reader in the form of a letter or a memorandum rather than as a separate document.

Whether the extended report is comparatively short or long, careful organisation of the information is still required to ensure that it is clear and logical to the reader. Therefore, this book will focus on the extended report rather than the form report.

i) Information reports

The first category of extended reports can be termed information reports. Here the main concern of the writer is to convey information to the reader often without any analysis of the facts.

Examples of information reports are:

Fact-finding reports in which the writer presents information that has been uncovered by thorough research. Very often this type of report answers the question 'What?' as in 'What are the main tourist attractions in Singapore?' The writer of this report will have to produce facts and figures to show the relative popularity of various tourist attractions. The figures may speak for themselves but here an analysis is necessary since a conclusion will be useful to highlight the main results and their significance.

What is a report?

Other 'what' reports may include: 'What are the goals of the department for the next three years?' 'What fringe benefits do our employees receive?' The title of your report may not include the word 'what', but in a fact-finding report you have to answer this question, maybe by listing and describing those goals, benefits, etc.

Annual reports present shareholders with the major facts concerning the operation of the company during the previous year, and its expectations for the year ahead. These reports can be regarded as being more than merely informative, because they aim to be persuasive in their presentation of information. Attractive photographs and charts convey the impression that the company is a professional one even if it is losing money.

Progress reports provide details of what has happened so far in an uncompleted job or project. For example, you may make an inspection of a construction site to find out if work is progressing according to schedule. It is essential that you record all problems that you observe, but the report may go beyond the informative since you may decide to recommend how the problems can be overcome.

ii) **Recommendation reports**

The second category of extended reports can be referred to as recommendation reports. The writer now has not only to analyse the information he has obtained and draw reasonable conclusions but also make appropriate recommendations. Examples are:

Feasibility reports. Before one goes ahead with a particular project, a feasibility report must be produced to answer the question 'Is this project feasible?'. 'Feasible' means not only possible but viable. If the completed project cannot recover the cost of construction a private company is unlikely to go ahead with it. The feasibility report will therefore draw conclusions from the information which will indicate how likely it is that the project will be a success. There is a bridge in England that was recently built across the River Humber. It is used by very few motorists and is an economic disaster. It would be interesting to read the feasibility report!

Problem-solving reports require a great deal of thought and analysis in order to find the best solution or solutions to a problem. If a company is being affected by lateness and absenteeism amongst the workers, then a report that addresses this problem would have to establish the seriousness of the problem and the reasons for it. Then it would be necessary to make recommendations based on the findings. Such recommendations may include an improvement in the working conditions in the factory, an increase in incentives, and/or disciplinary measures against offenders. The solutions that are suggested will act as a guide to management in the decisions they take to solve the problem.

There are many types of extended reports, but in the writing of each type the same principles apply and the finished product must exhibit the same qualities.

2 Before you start

If you refer to Chapter 1, you will see that our definition of a report includes these two essential phrases:

> **on a specific subject**
> **for a specific reader**

A SPECIFIC SUBJECT

Obviously you cannot write a report unless you have a subject to write about. A specific subject, however, suggests that you have a very clear understanding of the purpose of your report and of the areas that require investigation. This understanding is essential if you are going to write a successful report, and so you must obtain clear 'terms of reference' from the person who asks you to write the report.

TERMS OF REFERENCE

The terms of reference should state clearly the following information concerning the report:

- the purpose
- the scope
- the time limit for completing the report
- the person who is asking for the report
- the reader of the report

These terms of reference are to be found in the following memo.

From: The Personnel Officer
To: Mr. Low Kim Cheng
Date: 21 June 1988

The problem of absenteeism and lack of punctuality appears to be increasing. Please write a report that indicates the extent of the problem and the reasons for it. I should like to receive the report by 15 July so that it can be discussed at the next management committee meeting on 20 July.

P. Devaraj

PURPOSE

As a report writer you must know why you are writing your report and what you hope to achieve. In other words, your objectives must be clear in your own mind, otherwise you will never be sure whether or not you have successfully completed the report. To make sure that you do not overlook or misinterpret your objectives you ought to

write down your objectives clearly.

Referring to the above memo as your terms of reference you would write down:

Objectives

1. To examine the extent of the problem of absenteeism and lack of punctuality.
2. To determine the reasons for the problem.

Before you start

Now you should ask yourself the question **Do I know exactly what I have to do?**

If the answer is 'no', then the terms of reference are not clear and precise enough. How will you answer regarding the above example?

My answer is 'no'.

This means that you must get the personnel officer (the person who commissioned you to write the report) to clarify the objectives by asking him:

1. Do you want me to examine the problem of absenteeism and lack of punctuality throughout the company? Or are you only interested in the factory workers?

    Answer: 'Only the factory workers. The situation is satisfactory amongst the administrative staff.'

2. Do you want me to make any recommendations as to how this problem should be resolved?

    Answer: 'Yes, we must have appropriate recommendations.'

Now you can re-write your objectives.

Objectives

1. To examine the extent of the problem of absenteeism and lack of punctuality amongst the factory workers.
2. To determine the reasons for the problem.
3. To recommend how this problem can be resolved.

If the report reader expects a series of recommendations and you fail to produce them, he will blame you for not clarifying the objectives. If you write about all the employees of the company instead of the factory workers, you will have wasted your time. It only takes a telephone call or a memo to the person who commissioned you to sort out any doubts. Of course, he should have given you clear terms of reference in the first place. His memorandum should have read:

From: The Personnel Officer
To: Mr. Low Kim Cheng
Date: 21 June 1988

The problem of absenteeism and lack of punctuality amongst the **factory workers** appears to be increasing. Please write a report that indicates the extent of the problem and the reasons for it. Also make appropriate **recommendations** to resolve the problem. I should like to receive the report by 15 July so that it can be discussed at the next Management Committee Meeting on 20 July.

P. Devaraj

SCOPE

The scope indicates those areas which are to be covered in the report. Unless you know before you start your investigation which areas have to be considered you may make one of two mistakes.

1. You might include in your report information in which the reader is not interested, in which case you have wasted your time.

2. You might exclude information in which the reader is interested, in which case you will have a dissatisfied reader.

If the person who commissioned the above report on absenteeism and lack of punctuality had wanted a comparison with the situation two years earlier when another report had been written on the subject, this must be specified in the terms of reference.

The terms of reference need to be precise so that both the objectives and the scope of the report are clear. In 1987, a

Before you start

commission of enquiry was set up in Singapore to investigate a corruption case involving the late Mr Teh Cheang Wan when he was Minister for National Development. On completion of the enquiry, a report had to be written. You will notice that very precise terms of reference (see below) were drawn up to guide the commission so that no area that required investigation was omitted.

The Commission's terms of reference

1 To inquire whether:

a) THE Corrupt Practices Investigation Bureau (CPIB) did all that was necessary to uncover all the acts of corruption or criminal wrong-doing of the late Mr Teh Cheang Wan in investigating complaints of or leads to acts of corruption by the late Mr Teh Cheang Wan as Minister for National Development;

b) The CPIB was thorough in their investigations before concluding that there was no involvement by any other Minister, Parliamentary Secretary, or Government officer in these acts of corruption or other criminal wrong-doing;

c) There has been any attempt to overlook, to conceal or to cover-up any information concerning corruption or criminal wrong-doing.

2 To investigate:

a) Into the circumstances which made it possible for the former Minister for National Development to accept the two $400,000 bribes;

b) Whether other persons were involved or implicated in relation to the said two bribes or other bribes, if any;

c) The system used by the Ministry of National Development in:
i) Acquisition/alienation of land;
ii) Receiving and accepting of tenders; and
iii) The operations of its and related companies.

3 If the Commission finds:

(a) In respect of reference 2 (b) there were wrong-doings, then it shall refer the person or persons involved or implicated to the appropriate authorities;

(b) There are shortcomings in the system used by the Ministry of National Development and/or any of its or related companies, it shall receive proposals and make recommendations for their improvements and to prevent further corruption.

The Straits Times, 27 March 1987.

TIME LIMIT

The length of the report and its thoroughness will be affected by the amount of time you have to write it. The person who asked you to write the report must inform you when he wants it so that you can plan your work schedule accordingly. Try to keep to this schedule because if you are given prior notice of a deadline you have no excuse for producing a rushed piece of work or for requesting an extension.

A SPECIFIC READER

Remember that the reader is a **specific** reader (or group of readers). The report may be read by other interested people but you are writing the report for a specific reader and you must bear this in mind all the time. This reader may not be the person who is asking for the report for he may be passing it on to his superior. This superior is your specific reader.

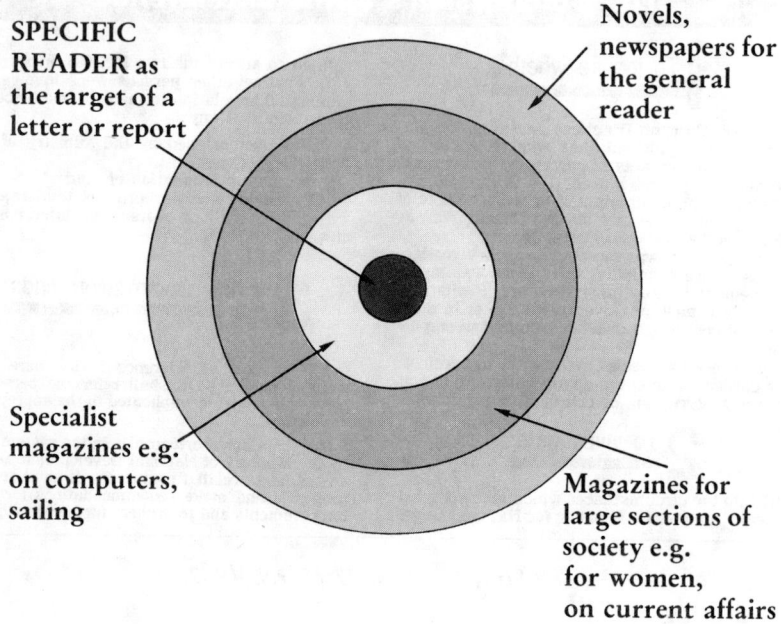

SPECIFIC READER as the target of a letter or report

Novels, newspapers for the general reader

Specialist magazines e.g. on computers, sailing

Magazines for large sections of society e.g. for women, on current affairs

KNOW THE READER

What do you need to know about the specific reader in relation to the report?

1. His situational knowledge of the subject.

    If he has only recently become involved in the project you will have to provide some background information to enable him to fully understand your report. On the other hand, if he knows about the project you would be wasting your time to give such details. You would also bore him.

2. **His technical knowledge of the subject.**

   You may be a specialist in a particular field but the reader may have only a basic knowledge of that field because he is either an administrator or an expert in a different field. Once you know the technical limitations of the reader you will have to use terminology that he will understand. Alternatively you could include a glossary to explain certain technical vocabulary. On the other hand if he is a technical expert you will not have to simplify your report at all.

3. **His opinions on the subject.**

   If you know that the reader has certain opinions and after your research and analysis you confirm that he is right, then you can expect your report to be favourably accepted. However, should you disagree with his opinion you would have to produce irrefutable evidence to make him change his mind. In other words, the reader's opinions will affect the amount of care and persuasiveness you put into your report.

By knowing these details about the reader you will be able to put yourself in his position and thus your report should be clearer, more concise and more convincing. Above all, the report must meet the requirements of the reader, and so you must be certain that you understand the objectives as stated in the terms of reference. Never hesitate to ask questions to clarify any doubts you may have. Such questions about either objectives or the reader can save a lot of time and will guide you in your research as well as in the actual writing of your report.

3 Getting the facts

Once you have established your objectives and certain details about the reader you can start your investigation. An investigation requires you to collect facts in order to build up a clear and accurate picture of the situation. You cannot, however, look randomly for information which might be of value. Instead you must think of the answers to these two questions:

>What facts do I need to obtain?
>How can I get these facts?

WHAT?

RELEVANT FACTS

The facts must be **relevant** to the purpose of the report. You will frequently find interesting information, but this can be ignored unless it is relevant.

ALL THE FACTS

If you obtain only half the facts you may have a distorted view of a situation. If you have definite ideas on a subject you may be tempted to find all the information that supports your opinion, and ignore the rest. This temptation must be avoided since your report should be objective, presenting all the facts so that the reader can make his own assessment based on all the evidence.

SPECIFIC FACTS

Generalisations are frequently an indication of insufficient research, e.g. 'Most of the factory workers arrive late from time to time.'

You must find out exact numbers and percentages of workers in relation to the frequency of their late arrival at work, e.g. '70 per cent of the factory workers arrive late at least twice a week.'

In order to find specific information you must start by deciding what facts you need to know. This can be done by adopting a **brainstorming** technique. Sit down for half an hour and, using the objectives as a guide, make a note of all the relevant facts that you would have to find out. You may come up with a list like this:

Absenteeism and lack of punctuality

1. Extent of problem

    i) Absenteeism
       - frequency
       - average no. of days
    ii) Lateness
       - frequency
       - average no. of minutes

2. Reasons

    i) for absence
       e.g. – personal matters to attend to
            – genuine ill health
            – dislikes job
            – dislikes conditions in factory
            – considers pay rather low
            – can't get along with fellow workers
    ii) for lateness
       e.g. – factory far from home
            – transportation problem
            – traffic congestion
            – dislikes job
            – feels no commitment to company

– no pay deduction for up to half hour late
– considers pay rather low

3. Comparison with situation two years ago

– Situation better or worse?
– Reasons similar or different?
– Have the recommendations of that report been implemented?
If so, are they successful?
If not, why not?

4. Possible recommendations

– to improve matters for workers e.g. incentives, transport
– to punish offenders e.g. pay deductions, sacking

This list will provide you with a framework to guide you in collecting the facts and planning the report. (See Chapter 4.)

HOW?

Having decided **what** facts you need to find out, you must now decide **how** you can obtain them. In other words, where will you get them from or to whom will you go? There are a variety of sources of information and they can be categorised according to the method of obtaining the information from each source.

- Reading
- Listening
- Experimenting
- Talking
- Observing
- Thinking

SOURCES OF INFORMATION

Reading. A vast amount of information is to be found in the written form. The report writer has to select what he thinks will be useful for his particular report. He can choose from the following:

Books will be especially important to project reports which students have to write.
Periodicals, journals provide the latest research findings whereas books can soon become out of date. An ability to use library catalogues is essential.
Acts, laws, regulations have to be checked to ensure that your proposal is legally permissible.
Newspapers provide accurate up-to-date information.
Files of correspondence, company records may have to be consulted for background information.
Reports that are related to yours can be consulted for the purpose of comparison or to obtain necessary information.

The above list is not exhaustive since there are so many types of written information. Some reports may require you to look at maps, drawings, timetables, brochures, etc. The list is endless, but you must decide which sources will be useful for your report.

Listening. There are a variety of sources of information that can be tapped by listening:

Lectures, seminars are particularly important for students.
Meetings, discussions at which people present facts and their opinions.
Television, radio may have a documentary related to the topic of your report.
Interviews require careful listening to ensure that you have understood exactly what the interviewee said.

Listening does not mean accepting everything that is said as factual. People may make assertions which are not supported by evidence. A good listener should be able to discriminate and read between the lines. The worker who tells you he does not wear the prescribed safety equipment because he keeps forgetting is most likely not telling the truth. He is either too lazy or he has a 'couldn't care less' attitude which may be the result of personal problems.

Experimenting. For certain reports, you will have to carry out your own experiments or tests. It goes without saying that you must make sure that the results are accurate.

Talking. Naturally you learn by listening rather than talking but sometimes it is necessary for you to provide the initial stimulus.

Observing. You may be told that the workers are taking long tea-breaks, but you need to confirm this, and so observation is necessary. Inspection reports in which you are examining a piece of equipment and progress reports require particularly careful observation.

Thinking. This last source of information is yourself. You have gained a certain amount of knowledge and experience over the years, and this must be used if it is appropriate to your report. As you think, you will be using your powers of analysis in evaluating the information you have collected. This evaluation will be discussed in greater detail in Chapter 4.

INTERVIEWS

Interviews have been mentioned briefly above, but it must be emphasised that the success of the interview, i.e. whether you obtain the information you require, depends largely on how skilful you are as an interviewer. Here are some suggestions as to how you should prepare for and conduct an interview.

Preparing for an interview.

1. **Know the purpose of the interview.**

    Unless you know what information you want to obtain you will not know when or if your interview has been successful. Nor will you even know when it is time to end the interview. A lot of time can be wasted by allowing an interview to go round in circles or to drag on indefinitely because you do not know whether you have obtained sufficient information.

Getting the facts

2. **Choose as an interviewee someone who can help you.**

    Take time to make sure you have found someone who can provide you with the information you need or else the interview will be very frustrating. Also give him some warning as to the kind of information you require so that he can come prepared.

3. **Prepare suitable questions.**

    Even experienced interviewers prepare questions in advance. But what makes a question 'suitable'?

    i) **Relevant.** The question should encourage the interviewee to give an answer which is informative and relevant to the subject of your report.

    ii) **Open-ended.** Too many closed questions, i.e. those that can be answered 'yes' or 'no', provide limited information which is black or white, whereas in life matters are rarely so clear-cut. For example, you may ask a supervisor, 'Do most of your workers arrive punctually at work?' He will probably answer 'yes'. Unless he continues to qualify this you will have learnt very little. It is better to ask an open-ended question which forces the supervisor to give you more precise information, e.g. 'How many of your workers arrive punctually at work each day?'

    iii) **Objective.** You want facts rather than opinions and so you should avoid questions which will lead to subjective answers. Avoid: 'What do you think of your workers' punctuality?' The answer 'OK' or 'Not very good' is subjective, not factual.

    iv) **Unbiased.** You should also avoid phrasing questions in such a way that the interviewee is persuaded to answer in the way you want. Avoid: 'Wouldn't you agree that many workers manage to get medical leave when they are not really ill?'

v) **Complete.** If you have prepared your questions well you should have no need to interview that person a second time. His answers should provide you with all the information you expected to obtain from him.

Conducting the interview

1. **Establish the right relationship.**

    A supervisor may feel ill at ease if he is being questioned by management, and so it is important that he can relax and concentrate on saying all he knows. Alternatively, if you are interviewing an expert or a superior you will have more confidence if you are well prepared and then you will be more likely to gain the respect and co-operation of the interviewee.

2. **Keep to the point.**

    Most people are very busy and so avoid too much chit-chat — have just enough at the beginning to establish some rapport. Try to prevent the interviewee from digressing by bringing him back to the question you have asked if he starts to wander off the point.

3. **Maintain eye contact.**

    This indicates you are dealing with a person rather than an information machine. If you are taking notes, look up from time to time, and always look up when you are speaking. This develops your rapport with the interviewee, encourages him to speak more and generally leads to a more interesting and informative interview.

4. **Speak clearly.**

    It is frustrating for the interviewee if he has to ask you to repeat a question.

Getting the facts

5. **Keep a record of the interview.**

    Jot down the key points or use a tape recorder to record the whole interview.
    (See Recording Information on Page 29.)

QUESTIONNAIRES

Questionnaires obtain information from a large number of people. Two questions from a travellers' survey illustrate how this information can be either factual:

Mode of Travel
Air (　) Sea (　) Road (　) Rail (　) Others (　)

or an expression of opinion:

How would you rate the service of

	Poor	Fair	Good	Please Specify
Immigration	(　)	(　)	(　)	....
Customs	(　)	(　)	(　)	....

In both cases it is important to consider the design of the questionnaire and the sample of people who will be asked to complete it.

Design

The questionnaire must be designed so that the information that is obtained is relevant, accurate and can be analysed to draw conclusions for your report.

1. **Decide what information you want.**

    You cannot start formulating questions until you know the objectives of the questionnaire. Since these objectives are related to those of your report, you will be seeking specific information that will directly assist you in your report.

2. **Explain to the respondents the purpose of the questionnaire.**

   A short introduction will give the respondents a better understanding of the questionnaire and should make them more interested in it and more willing to give thought to their answers.

3. **Give clear instructions.**

   The respondents must know what they are supposed to do, and so the instructions need to be simple and unambiguous.

4. **Make the questionnaire user-friendly.**

   Your questions as well as your instructions must be clear. Sometimes a questionnaire is intended for a small group of people who have time to complete it in detail, but the majority of questionnaires are completed by many people who have little time to do so. The latter type of questionnaire must be user-friendly otherwise the respondents may misinterpret your questions. Another aspect of user-friendliness is the form of the questions. Occasionally you may want written comments that express the respondents' opinions, but most questions will be of the 'Tick the appropriate box' type, e.g.

   How often do you go to the cinema?

Once a year	☐	Once a month	☐
Twice a year	☐	Twice a month	☐
Once every 3 months	☐	Once a week	☐

   The boxes could be marked

Never	☐	Quite frequently	☐
Seldom	☐	Frequently	☐
Occasionally	☐		

Which of these two examples provides information that is more precise? The first one. It also gives more information. For instance, in the second example, what do you understand by 'occasionally' — is it once a month or once every three months? The answer is purely subjective and therefore your analysis of the data will not be totally accurate.

Unfortunately questionnaires generally suffer from subjectivity and this cannot be avoided when opinions are sought, such as when determining the quality of a person or a product, e.g.

Rate your seminar leader on a scale from 1 to 5 where 1 is the lowest and 5 the highest. Circle the appropriate number.

1.	He has a good knowledge of the subject.	1	2	3	4	5
2.	He explains his material clearly.	1	2	3	4	5
3.	He makes the seminar interesting.	1	2	3	4	5
4.	He is willing to answer questions.	1	2	3	4	5
5.	He has a good rapport with the group.	1	2	3	4	5

By making the questionnaire user-friendly you are increasing the chances of getting the co-operation of the respondent and thus the accuracy of the data you obtain.

5. **Ask relevant questions.**

Naturally the questions should be relevant to the objectives of the questionnaire. Avoid digressing even if a question that comes to mind seems interesting. You do not want irrelevant data.

6. **Make sure the results can be analysed.**

'Tick a box' questions can be analysed easily by adding up the ticks for each box. Conclusions can be drawn when certain boxes have been ticked either by a clear majority or very few of the respondents.

Open-ended questions, however, can lead to an infinite number of answers which cannot be analysed easily. e.g.

> What do you think of Changi Airport?

Such a question is too vague and therefore of little value. Nevertheless, when the number of respondents is not too large, such as for the questionnaire on the seminar, it is useful to have a final question such as

> Other comments ....

These comments can highlight certain points or indicate new areas not covered in the questionnaire.

7. **Make sure the questionnaire is well organised.**

If the questionnaire covers more than one topic, take each one in turn. For example, if you are rating a seminar you must consider the leader, the materials and the methodology. Design a set of questions on one topic before moving to the next. Within each category it is usually best to start with general questions and then move on to the specific. The organisation of the questionnaire must be logical to the respondent.

Fig. 3.1 provides a sample questionnaire that might be used by a company conducting a market research on office furniture to find out the ratio of wood-based furniture to non-wood based furniture.

This is a detailed questionnaire which will provide a lot of useful information. However, it requires thought and time to complete it accurately.

Fig. 3.2 can be completed much more quickly since it is aimed at the visitor to Malaysia who would not be willing to spend as much time on the questionnaire as the executive who is being asked directly by a researcher to complete it.

The length of the questionnaire must be related not only to the objectives but also to the people who will be required to complete it.

Getting the facts

It is sometimes said that questionnaires are used by people to provide evidence to support their own point of view. This can be done by leading the respondents with biased questions, but this approach should be avoided when collecting information for an objective report.

Sample

The sample selected for the questionnaire must be representative. Thus if you are conducting a questionnaire amongst the factory workers of a large company you would have to choose workers from different sections, of different ages, of both sexes. When I see people at Holland Village (a shopping area in Singapore frequented by many expatriates) conducting surveys I often wonder how representative their sample is since the high percentage of expatriates is not a true reflection of the whole of Singapore.

RECORDING INFORMATION

It is important that you record the information you find in an organised manner so that you can locate a specific piece of information quickly as you plan and write your report. The notes you make from your research should be recorded in the following way:

1. **Write down the necessary details of books** such as the title, author, publisher, date and place of publication. If it is a periodical, also state the volume number, page reference and the titles of both the periodical and the article.

    If in your report you quote from a book you will have to state the source and give the page number, and so record page numbers in your notes to avoid having to refer to the book again.

2. **Write on only one side of your sheet of paper.** This can make planning easier. (See Chapter 4.)

3. **Highlight headings** using a highlighter pen or capitals. You may use your own headings which indicate how these notes relate to the subject of your report.

The Complete Asian Report Writer

Project: Office furniture
Main questionnaire

1. Can we go through this furniture first together, item by item and tell me approximately how many of each item your office currently has? Out of this total number, can you estimate the number of each item which has got some wood that you can actually see (that means that would be partly or totally wood-based vs those which is totally non-wood based?) for eg steel filing cabinets would be non wood-based and wooden chairs would be wood-based.

	Furniture items	Total n %	'Wood-based' (wood related partially or wholly) n %	Non-wood related n %
i)	**Tables**			
	Executive tables			
	Administration/typist tables/Typist trolley			
	Conference table			
	Side/coffee table			
ii)	**Chairs**			
	Swivel/can rotate			
	Non-swivel/Fixed			
iii)	Built in book shelves/racks			
iv)	Built in cabinets/cupboards			
v)	Built in partitions			
vi)	Moveable book shelves/racks			
vii)	Moveable cabinets/cupboards			
viii)	Moveable partitions			
ix)	Settee/sofa			
x)	**Antique wooden furniture**			
	o chairs			
	o tables			
	o screens			
	o others ————			
xi)	Other furniture items (specify) ————			

Fig. 3.1 A detailed questionnaire a

Getting the facts

2. Below here are some things that your might look for in deciding to buy your office furniture. Would you please look at these factors and then rate them in importance from 1 point (not important) to 10 points (very important). Also rank them in the order of your importance from 15 (most important) to 1 (least important).

		Rating (1-10 pts)	Ranking order (15-1)
a.	Quality	_____	_____
b.	Durability	_____	_____
c.	Design/style of furniture (traditional, modern, classic)	_____	_____
d.	Exclusive ie not commonly found in your offices	_____	_____
e.	Practicality/convenience of usage (?)	_____	_____
f.	Comfort	_____	_____
g.	Well matched/well coordinated design	_____	_____
h.	Feature where you can have additional sets added to your existing set which are matched eg open plan system	_____	_____
i.	Delivery time of the furniture that you ordered	_____	_____
j.	After sales service for repair/maintenance/re-upholstering	_____	_____
k.	Guarantee on wear and tear (for eg one year)	_____	_____
l.	Brandname of the furniture	_____	_____
m.	Reputation of the company that manufactures it	_____	_____
n.	Imported	_____	_____
o.	Bulk or quantity discount	_____	_____

b

3a.   Currently are you satisfied with your office furniture in general ?

                        YES   1
                        NO   2   -   Ask   7b

3b.   Why are you not satisfied ? What furniture units would you like to get improved ? Why ?

        _____
        _____
        _____

4a.   In your own opinion, do you foresee any possible future purchase of furniture items in your office ?

                        YES   1 — 8 b
                        NO   2

4b.   What might these furniture items be ?

        _____
        _____

Getting the facts

5. Have you any suggestions on any new types of furniture that would help make your own office <u>more attractive</u> and <u>more efficient</u> ? Anything at all to upgrade the current standard of office furniture ?

   _____
   _____
   _____

6. Normally when an order has been placed on the furniture item, what is the duration of time (days/weeks) involved from the time an order was placed to the delivery of furniture to your office.

   Duration of time : _____ (Days/Weeks)

Fig. 3.2 A straightforward questionnaire

Getting the facts

1. Date of arrival .... Date of departure ....
2. Nationality .... Country of Residence ....
3. Mode of Travel

   Air ( )   Sea ( )   Road ( )   Rail ( )   Others ( )

4. Sources of Information on Malaysia
   - Own experience ( )   Travel Agents ( )   Airline/Shipping Co. ( )
   - TDC Office ( )   Guide Book ( )   Magazine/Newspapers ( )
   - Others (Please Specify): ....

5. Did you encounter any problems in obtaining an entry visa to Malaysia (except for employment).
   If so, please specify ....

6. How would you rate the service of:-

	Poor	Fair	Good	Please Specify
Immigration	( )	( )	( )	....
Customs	( )	( )	( )	....

7. How would you assess air accessibility to Malaysia.

   (a) Choice of flights (different times & days)   Poor ( ) Fair ( ) Good ( )
   (b) Choice of types of flight (non-stop & direct, etc) Poor ( ) Fair ( ) Good ( )

   Any other comments on accessibility ....

8. How do you rate Malaysia on the following:-

	Poor	Fair	Good	Please Specify
Friendliness	( )	( )	( )	....
Accommodation	( )	( )	( )	....
Food	( )	( )	( )	....
Cleanliness	( )	( )	( )	....
Culture/History	( )	( )	( )	....
Shopping	( )	( )	( )	....
Attractions	( )	( )	( )	....
Sightseeing (tours etc.)	( )	( )	( )	....
Traffic	( )	( )	( )	....
Public Amenities	( )	( )	( )	....

   Local Transportation

	Poor	Fair	Good	
Air	( )	( )	( )	....
Rail	( )	( )	( )	....
Bus	( )	( )	( )	....
Taxi	( )	( )	( )	....
Car Rental	( )	( )	( )	....

   Hotels

	Poor	Fair	Good	Please Specify
Hospitality	( )	( )	( )	
Food	( )	( )	( )	
Services/Facilities	( )	( )	( )	
Environment	( )	( )	( )	
Room Rates	( )	( )	(	

9. Any additional comments, if any: ....
   ....

4. Taking notes is more difficult when you are interviewing someone, and so it is a good idea to **use a tape recorder**, providing you obtain the interviewee's permission first. Then you can concentrate on what he is saying and ask relevant follow-up questions where appropriate.

If the interviewee refuses permission you will have to jot down the main points and then **immediately** after the interview expand on those notes whilst the information you gained from the interviewee is still fresh in your mind. If you wait, you will forget certain facts.

Remember to **write down the name of the person** you interviewed. If he is an expert expressing his view or a witness stating what happened you will have to refer to him by name in your report.

Example

How will you obtain the facts for the report on 'absenteeism and lack of punctuality amongst the factory workers'?

Reading:
Other report(s)
Company regulations
Wage structure for workers
Records of workers
Details of public transport available e.g. bus timetables

Observing:
Workers' punctuality
Traffic congestion
Conditions in the factory
Attitudes of the workers

Talking/Listening:
Interview supervisors
Interview a few workers
Questionnaire for all workers
Interview finance director regarding existing and potential penalties and incentives.

Thinking: Use your own knowledge of the situation and of psychology to evaluate the information you obtain from the workers, and to assist you in deciding whether penalties for offenders or incentives for punctual, regular workers would be the best solution.

SUMMARY

A successful report requires hard thinking and careful research in order to obtain the necessary relevant information. Start by thinking about **what** information you will need and then how you can obtain it. Use all possible sources which may mean you will have to do some **reading, listening, experimenting, talking, observing and thinking.**

Look for **specific** facts which will provide you with all the relevant information you need to make your report complete and objective. Do not rely on your memory but write down your findings, together with the source of the information, so that you will be able to organise your findings more easily when you start planning your report.

4 Planning the report

There are **four** basic sections in a report:

- the Introduction
- the Body (which contains the findings)
- the Conclusion
- the Recommendations

The order in which these sections appear in your report is discussed in detail in Chapter 8. The primary purpose of this chapter is to explain how to plan the body of the report so that the relevant information is communicated clearly to the reader. There will be a more detailed analysis of the Introduction in Chapter 5, while the Conclusion and the Recommendations will be discussed in Chapters 8 and 9 respectively.

In an extended formal report there will be a table of contents which will indicate how the report has been organised. Below is an example of a **table of contents** from a market research report on the impact of various advertisements for a particular product.

INTRODUCTION

The essential components of the introduction are:

- the objectives as stated in the terms of reference
- the background information that the specific reader may require to help him understand the whole report
- the method of enquiry to show how you obtained the information.

Planning the report

> **CONTENTS**
>
> A. **INTRODUCTION**
>
> 1. Background
> 2. Objectives
> 3. Method
>
> B. **FINDINGS**
>
> 1. Impact and branding
> 2. Communication
> 3. Detailed recall of content
> 4. Likes and dislikes
> 5. Prompted comments
> 6. Brand/product images
> 7. Likelihood of buying
>
> C. **CONCLUSION**
>
> D. **RECOMMENDATIONS**

Fig 4.1 Table of contents

In this chapter we are discussing how to organise the facts, and so we need to consider the question 'What facts go in the background?'.

The background should be kept as brief as possible, explaining the need for the report, which often requires a description of a problem that needs to be examined. The amount of factual information to be included depends on the reader's situational and technical knowledge of the subject of the report. The less he knows, the more you must include so that he will have no difficulty understanding the findings. The background, however, must not contain any findings. These go in the body of the report.

39

BODY/FINDINGS

You have obtained all the facts necessary to make your report complete. These facts now need to be arranged to form the body of the report. Since the body of the report presents all the necessary information it is important that the information is arranged in such a way that the reader will be able to understand the report easily. In other words it must be clear to him at the first reading. To achieve such clarity you need to pay attention to

- the **selection** of information
- the **organisation** of information
- the **ordering** of information

SELECTION

You will have collected a great deal of information during your research, but not all of it will be included in your report. You will have to evaluate the information to establish whether it is:

- Relevant
- Unbiased
- Accurate
- Up to date

Relevant. In spite of efforts to ensure that you have collected only relevant facts you will discover that at times you are not quite sure whether the information will prove to be relevant or not. Now as you plan the body of the report you must decide whether a specific piece of information is to be included because it is relevant or omitted. But what is meant by **relevant**? It means 'connected with the subject' (*Longman Dictionary of Contemporary English*). In report writing we need to be more precise and say that relevant means 'connected with the purpose of the report'. In addition it is important to remember the reader, so that the selection of information is guided by what he needs and wants to know.

Example

As you conduct the investigation for the report on absenteeism and lack of punctuality among the workers, you learn that when the Singapore Mass Rapid Transit railway is completed in 1990, there will be a station within 2 km of the factory. Is this relevant to your report?

YES	NO
It might help solve the problem of lack of punctuality.	It is not a reason for absenteeism or lack of punctuality.
	The MRT will be of use to a small number of employees only.
	Definite solutions are needed now — possible part-solutions for two years' time are of no value.

It would appear from the above evaluation that this specific piece of information is not directly relevant to the purpose. Therefore you should omit it.

Unbiased. As you obtain information it is likely that some of it will be biased because the writer is trying to prove a point even though he lacks sufficient evidence. In his desperation he may even distort some evidence. This writer is not presenting **facts**, but his **opinions** and opinions are never totally objective since we are all affected by personal desires, moods, circumstances, peer pressure etc. Therefore, as a report writer searching for facts you must take care that you do not accept as fact a piece of information that is only an opinion. Here are some guidelines to help you make this distinction.

1. **Read critically**

   Do not accept as fact everything you read. Look for evidence to support any claims a writer is making and decide whether he has misinterpreted or ignored certain vital evidence.

2. **Listen critically**

Make sure the interviewee you select knows about the subject which you are researching. If it is a technical report he must be an expert in the appropriate area of specialisation. Then listen critically to him, noting if he has proof of statements he is making or merely presenting his theories as if they were really true.

3. **Beware of questionnaires**

Questionnaires that ask for opinions are not totally accurate. If the questionnaire is completed anonymously respondents may take the opportunity to complain, often exaggerating the situation. On the other hand if they have to give their names they may be afraid to be critical. In both cases there will be inaccurate results. However if a large percentage of the respondents hold a certain view, you should accept this as significant.

4. **Beware of advertising**

It is part of advertising to present a piece of information as if it were a proven fact, e.g. 'Tests have proved that our petrol burns more cleanly.'

It is interesting that each petrol company has conducted tests to prove that its petrol is the best! Do you really believe all the claims of advertisements? Try to distinguish between a fact and a claim.

Fact or opinion?

What do you think?

1. Japanese cars are better than European ones.
2. Japanese cars are cheaper than European ones.
3. The recent advertising campaign has been extremely successful.
4. Our toothpaste gives you double protection.

Planning the report

5. According to the site foreman, construction is behind schedule owing to bad weather last month.

Answers:

1. Opinion. 'Better' is a quality judgement based on people's opinions. With so many models available a true comparison of quality is not feasible.
2. Fact. Price can be compared, so this is a fact assuming you have obtained evidence.
3. Fact. Proof can be obtained to show that sales have increased.
4. Opinion. This sounds like an advertisement.
5. Opinion. To change this to a fact more research is necessary to establish how many days it rained.

Accurate. Your facts must be accurate, but sometimes you may obtain conflicting information, and then you have to take action to establish the truth of the situation.

Example

You work at the head office of a chain of supermarkets. Head Office has recently received a number of complaints from customers about the long time they have to queue at the check-out counters because several of these counters are not manned. You investigate by interviewing the managers and cashiers at the different supermarkets. The former state that all the check-out counters are manned throughout the day except for lunch-time from 12 – 2 pm and dinner-time from 6 – 8 pm. The cashiers, however, say that there is often one that is unmanned for most of the day. Now you must use a different technique of obtaining information — that of **observation.** You may tend to believe the cashiers because they are on the spot whereas the manager is in his office, but proof comes by observation.

Up to date. Make sure that the statistics you have obtained are the most recent ones. Sales can rise or fall dramatically within a short period of time.

It should be apparent that during your **selection** of information you may realise that you need to carry out further research to fill in one or two gaps in the information you have already collected. You would be wrong though to think that **planning** occurs only after you have completed your research. You must also be evaluating information and organising it whilst you are collecting the facts, but eventually you must make the final decision on what to include and the best way to present it.

ORGANISATION

The table of contents (Fig 4.1) illustrates how the findings can be organised under seven different headings. Two questions need to be answered:

> **Why organise the findings under headings?**
> **How do I do this?**

WHY?

Headings are essential in every report for the following reasons:

1. **They increase the report's readability.**

   Imagine a printed page without any breaks. Reading such a page is quite a daunting prospect because you do not know the topic, nor where each topic starts and finishes. Headings guide the reader through the report, splitting it up into manageable sections.

2. **They provide the reader with an overview of the report.**

   The headings in the report match the table of contents and so they indicate to the reader the areas that are going to be considered and their sequence.

3. **They help the reader to read selectively.**

   If the reader is interested in only one aspect of your report he can easily locate the relevant information without having to scan the whole report.

4. **They help the reader to understand the details.**

   Once he knows the topic of a particular section the reader will anticipate the information that is going to be presented. This anticipation means he is better prepared to understand the details.

5. **They show the reader where to stop and think.**

   The reader should read critically, thinking about whether the information is relevant and complete, and then drawing his own conclusions. The moment for such reflection is at the end of a section.

6. **They make the report more concise.**

   Without headings to indicate the start of each new section there would have to be transition passages to tell the reader that you have finished discussing one topic and are now moving on to the next, e.g.

   > 'Those are the reasons for absenteeism amongst the workers. Now let us consider the reasons for lack of punctuality.'

   With headings, such transition passages must be omitted.

If a topic can be divided into sections then you should have sub-headings which all relate to the main heading. This increases the benefits of headings as explained above.

Fig. 4.2 is an example of headings and sub-headings for a feasibility report on the setting up of a private educational establishment. Note how the sub-headings are related to the main heading. In a longer report the heading 'Findings' is generally omitted, and the word 'Body' is **never** used as a heading.

CONTENTS

1. INTRODUCTION

    1.1 Objectives
    1.2 Scope
    1.3 Background

2. ORGANISATION

    2.1 Legal entity
    2.2 Governing body
    2.3 Academic organisation
    2.4 Administrative organisation

3. FINANCE

    3.1 Funding
    3.2 Cost

4. ACADEMIC BODY

    4.1 Numbers
    4.2 Sources of staff
    4.3 Qualifications
    4.4 Academic salaries

5. STUDENT BODY

    5.1 Full-time day students
    5.2 Part-time day students
    5.3 Evening students

6. CURRICULUM, TIMETABLE etc.

    6.1 Curriculum
    6.2 Timetable
    6.3 Contact hours

> 6.4   Examinations
> 6.5   Qualifications
>
> 7.   CONCLUSION
>
> 8.   RECOMMENDATION

Fig. 4.2 Headings and sub-headings in a table of contents.

HOW?

How do I organise the findings under headings?

1. **Read through your notes** and write down the topic of each note in the margin. You now have a series of headings.

2. **'Sort and group'** is a technique which is often recommended. Write out the headings into a list and decide which ones can be grouped together. These may form a series of sub-headings to which you have to add a main heading. Alternatively you may find that the main heading is obvious and you need to decide which topics relate to it.

3. **Check with the original outline** that you made before starting the research (See Page 19). There is likely to be some similarity, but the new plan (with sub-headings) will probably be more detailed.

4. **Check the headings and sub-headings carefully** to make sure that they clearly describe the topic that you intend to discuss or present information about. Each heading should
   - cover the scope of information to be included in that section
   - not overlap with the scope indicated by the other headings
   - be clear

- be precise
- be brief (subject to the above)

Remember too that sub-headings should refer to the heading itself. (See Fig. 4.2)

ORDERING

Now that the information has been grouped you need to decide on the sequence in which you are going to present it. Which section will come first, next and last? The sequence must be the most logical one for the particular report you are writing.

What is a 'logical order' in a report?

This depends on the type of report you are writing. For a progress report a chronological order (i.e. according to time order) is generally the most appropriate. Thus for a technical progress report your headings may be:

Work completed (since last report)
Work scheduled (during next period)
Work proposed (for the future)

A similar structure may be employed by a salesman who reports on:

Last month's performance
This month's schedule
Future plans and expectations

For an information report the most important information is presented first since this will be read first by the reader, whose attention you are attempting to gain. Should he find the first topic insignificant he may read no further.

A well-organised report is clear to the reader. As he follows your line of thought he is more likely to agree with your conclusions. In addition he will realise you have given considerable thought to the issues involved and will be impressed by your clear thinking. A report writer who can present his findings clearly by means of a well-structured plan has a bright future.

Planning the report

The logical sequence is clarified by the use of a **numbering system,** as illustrated in Figs. 4.1 and 4.2. The most commonly used numbering system is the one shown in Fig. 4.2, which is the decimal system.

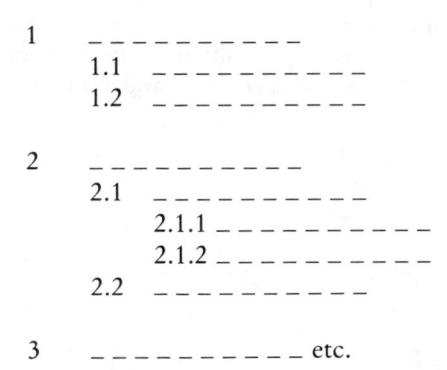

```
1     _____
      1.1   _____
      1.2   _____

2     _____
      2.1   _____
            2.1.1 _____
            2.1.2 _____
      2.2   _____

3     _____ etc.
```

Note that sub-headings are indented. This enables the reader to see clearly the main headings as distinct from the sub-headings. Similarly the sub-sub-headings, which refer to the sub-heading, are further indented. Thus the numbering system shows how the headings, sub-headings and sub-sub-headings are inter-related. Apart from the decimal system which uses Arabic numerals alone, one can also use letters and/or Roman numerals.

```
A     _____              I     _____
      1   _____                A   _____
      2   _____                B   _____

B     _____              II    _____
      1   _____                A   _____
      2   _____                B   _____
            (a) _____              (i)  _____
            (b) _____              (ii) _____

C     _____              III   _____
```

The numbering system also provides a convenient method of reference during any discussion of the report. Referring a colleague to a particular section number is quick and clear.

Example

PHOTOGRAPHY FOR DRAWINGS

Your company makes use of photographs in the preparation of outline or location drawings for its manuals. You must write a report that examines the present method of obtaining photographs and investigate the possibility of a more efficient and economical method.

Here are the main points you have recorded in your notes:

End December 1985:

— closure of company's photographic dept.

From 1986 to the present:

— used local professional photographer.

- Takes 5 working days to get photographs back.
- Transport cost $15 per visit.
- High quality photographs, too high for our needs.
- Cost of photographs: $100 per set of 10 (not including transport)
- Have to fit in with photographer's schedule.
- Took 500 photographs in 1986; 10 per visit i.e. once a week. Drawings of equipment done from photographs.
- Cost due to personnel time in supervising photographer $20 per visit.
- For a company of our size and status to rely totally on one photographer is not a good idea.
- Administrative cost (paperwork, secretarial time, stamps) $200 per annum.
- Can take own photographs and enlarge photographs to required size for drawings using own photocopier.
- Cost per photocopy: 5 cents.
- Can take photographs whenever we need to.
- Cost of buying camera, lenses and lights: $2000, but will last 10 yrs.
- Cost of 10 photographs: $15.
- Can develop photographs immediately.

Planning the report

- No difference in personnel time.
- Take equipment to photographer to save on transport cost. Cheaper to use company car — but not necessarily available when needed.

STEP 1: SELECTION

Cross out whatever is irrelevant or subjective.

~~For a company of our size and status to rely totally on one local photographer is not a good idea.~~

It is not clear how this note could be relevant to the report. In any case it is the writer's idea, in other words an opinion, since it could be argued that it is good to have a link with the local business community, or that it all depends on how efficient the photographer is.

STEP 2: ORGANISING

a) Label each note with an appropriate heading to indicate what it is about.

Background:	End December 1985 — closure of company's photographic dept.
Present method:	From 1986 to the present — used local professional photographer.
Delay:	Takes 5 working days to get photographs back.
Cost of transport:	Transport costs $15 per visit.
Quality:	High quality photographs, too high for our needs.
Cost of photos:	Cost of photographs: $100 per set of 10 (not including transport).

Inconvenience:	Have to fit in with photographer's schedule.
Method of operation:	Took 500 photographs in 1986; 10 per visit i.e. once per week. Drawings of equipment done from photographs.
Personnel cost:	Cost due to personnel time in supervising photographer $20 per visit.
	~~For a company of our size and status to rely totally on one local photographer is not a good idea.~~
Admin. cost:	Administration cost (paperwork, secretarial time, stamps) $200 p.a.
Method of operation:	Can take own photographs and enlarge photographs to required size for drawings using own photocopier.
Cost of photocopying:	Cost per photocopy: 5 cents.
Convenience:	Can take photographs whenever we need to.
Cost of camera etc:	Cost of buying camera, lenses and lights: $2000, but will last 10 yrs.
Cost of photos:	Cost of 10 photographs: $15
Speed of developing:	Can develop photographs immediately.
Personnel cost:	No difference in personnel time.
Benefits/problems of amendment to present method:	Take equipment to photographer to save on transport cost. Cheaper to use company car — but not necessarily available when needed.

b) Arrange the headings into groups.

Background

Present method   **Alternative method**
Delay   Method of operation

Planning the report

    Cost of transport   Cost of camera etc.
    Quality   Cost of photocopying
    Cost of photos   Convenience
    Inconvenience   Cost of photos
    Method of operation   Personnel cost
    Personnel cost   Speed of developing photo-
                                                  graphs

    Admin. cost
    Benefits/problems of taking equipment to photographer i.e. possible amendment to present method

c) Arrange sub-groups within each group, changing the headings where necessary, adding a main heading, or combining headings that overlap.

Background

Present method

    Inconvenience ⎫
                         ⎬ Disadvantages
    Delay   ⎭
    Cost
          – Transport
          – Photographs
          – Personnel
          – Admin.
    Method of Operation*
    Possible Amendment to Present Method

Proposed method
    Cost
          – camera etc.
          – photocopying
          – photographs
          – personnel

Convenience
Speed of developing photographs } Advantages

* 'Quality' can be included in the 'Method of Operation' as it contributes to a description of the present procedure.

STEP 3: ORDERING

Put the headings in the most logical sequence, so that you have a clear plan for your report.

1. INTRODUCTION
   1.1 Purpose
   1.2 Background

2. PRESENT METHOD
   2.1 Method of operation
   2.2 Cost
      2.2.1 Photographs
      2.2.2 Transport
      2.2.3 Personnel
      2.2.4 Administration
      2.2.5 Total
   2.3 Disadvantages
      2.3.1 Inconvenience
      2.3.2 Delay in receiving photographs
   2.4 Possible amendment

3. PROPOSED METHOD
   3.1 Method of operation
   3.2 Cost
      3.2.1 Camera, lenses etc.
      3.2.2 Photographs
      3.2.3 Photocopying
      3.2.4 Personnel
      3.2.5 Total
   3.3 Advantages
      3.3.1 Convenience
      3.3.2 Speed of developing photographs

4. CONCLUSION

5. RECOMMENDATION

You will observe that the above plan is symmetrical in that the sub-headings under each section of the findings — The Present Method and The Proposed Method — are similar. This indicates clear thinking on the part of the report writer and enables a comparison to be made very easily so that the conclusions that are drawn are seen to be logical.

The presentation of information is in a logical order because:

i) The reader needs to know details of the present method before he learns of any alternatives.
ii) An understanding of the Method of Operation is necessary first so that the reader can appreciate the various costs involved and the advantages/disadvantages.
iii) The essential costs are placed first.

APPENDICES

Sometimes you will find information which is partly relevant. A long table of statistics may contain a few relevant figures, or a letter taken from the files of correspondence may provide you with a vital statement that proves your point. Are you going to include the whole table or the whole letter in the body of your report?

The solution is to make use of **appendices.** In the body of the report you state the vital information provided by the figures or letter, and refer the reader to an appendix where he can see the whole table or whole letter if he is interested. The decision whether to include the whole table in the body or in the appendix is based on the question

Is it essential for the reader to examine the whole table to fully understand the report?

YES: Put the table in the body.
NO: Put the table in an appendix.

The Complete Asian Report Writer

If the answer is 'no', but you put the table in the body it will have a negative effect on the reader's grasp of the essential information. It will slow down his reading speed.

Each appendix should be labelled Appendix A, or Appendix B etc., and referred to in the body. Therefore, do not just add an appendix because you are not sure whether the information is relevant or not. Decisions on relevancy must be taken at the **selection** stage. Here we are thinking **where** to put the information.

Fig. 4.1 shows the outline of a market research report. As one would expect, this report is based on the results of a questionnaire. Consequently the detailed results of this questionnaire are placed at the back of the report as an appendix. Fig. 4.3 shows a table which is referred to in Section 1 of the Findings with the heading 'Impact and branding'.

```
              RECALL OF ADVERTISEMENTS FROM REEL
```

	Recalled Recalled at all %	Recalled brand name %	Recalled in 1st 3 positions %	Mean recall position
Air Canada	78	71	67	1.77
Shell Oil	64	44	49	2.66
Cadbury's Caramel	69	59	41	3.33
American Express	44	40	21	3.89
Fresh Cream Cakes	45	42	13	4.39
Sunkist Oranges	53	49	19	4.03
Nestle's Double Top	69	30	33	3.84
Mothers Pride	27	24	7	5.03
British Bacon	59	42	20	4.56
Campari	62	52	15	4.74

(124)

Fig. 4.3 Results of a questionnaire given as an appendix.

Planning the report

The report outlined in Fig. 4.2 contained 21 appendices at the end of a report of 45 pages. The essential information is contained in the 45 pages, but the appendices contain further details if the reader wishes to refer to them. Twenty-one is a large number of appendices, but each one is relevant.

Section 4.4 'Academic salaries' contains these paragraphs:

> 'Salary scales have been devised which give generous remuneration, designed to obtain full commitment from the staff. These scales are detailed in Appendix H.
>
> Additions to the basic scale have been set up to recognise academic qualifications and years of experience in teaching.'

The details have been put in the appendix and the explanations in the body.

There is frequently more than one way of planning your report, but you need to decide which plan will present your information and conclusions most clearly and logically to the reader. Since it is important for him to be able to follow your line of thinking without any distractions, appendices serve a vital function.

CONCLUSION/RECOMMENDATIONS

As mentioned at the beginning of this chapter, these sections will be considered in detail in later chapters. It must be noted though that the conclusion must contain logical deductions based on the information presented in the body. These deductions lead logically on to the recommendations. In other words, the whole report must follow a logical progression so that the reader can understand clearly how you reached your conclusions and recommendations.

5 Writing the introduction

The introduction section of a report serves two main purposes:

1. To provide the reader with any information that he will need to know in order to understand fully the body of the report.

2. To prevent the reader from expecting something that the report does not contain.

Both of these purposes focus on the reader because any written business communication is intended to be read by an individual or a specific group of people. The report writer's task is to ensure that the report will be clear to the specific reader, and in addition he wants to prevent people from reading the details only to discover that the report is not relevant to their particular purpose.

Part of the introduction is based on the terms of reference which are explained in Chapter 2. This is because the reader, like the report writer, needs to know the purpose and the scope from the outset.

What are the various parts of the introduction?

1. **Purpose**

   Tell the reader immediately what you are setting out to achieve through your report. If you have more than one objective, you must state all of them. This will enable the reader to understand why certain facts have been included and how you have reached your conclusions.

2. Recommendation

One objective may be to make a specific recommendation, such as the most suitable computer system to install, or a list of recommendations perhaps stating necessary action to overcome a problem.

The purpose/recommendation section of the introduction may be written as follows:

> This report examines the extent of the problem of absenteeism and lack of punctuality amongst the factory workers. It investigates the reasons for the problem and recommends measures that could be taken to resolve it.

3. Scope

'Scope' is 'the range of something' (*Oxford Universal Dictionary*). The reader needs to know the range of subjects that are going to be covered in the report, and what information is not going to be included. In this way the scope will help to inform the reader whether the contents of the report will provide him with the information he is seeking.

The scope of a report on 'The most suitable alternative to fossil fuels as a source of energy for Singapore in the 1990s', may be:

> 'The three alternatives to fossil fuels considered in this report are solar energy, wind power and hydro-power.'

One aspect of scope is an answer to the question 'What are the limitations or restrictions concerning the subject matter of this report?'

> 'This report considers only the economic aspects of the proposal.'

You may also wish to add the reason for these restrictions:

> 'This report does not include information relating to our

exports outside the Asia-Pacific region since this will be the subject of another report.'

An example of the scope, including the range and limitations of the report is:

> 'The three alternatives to fossil fuels considered in this report are solar energy, wind power and hydro-power. The omission of other alternatives is due to the excessive dangers involved in utilising these sources, such as nuclear power, or to the obvious inability of the source to provide sufficient energy to meet the needs of Singapore in the 1990s.'

4. **Background or problem**

The background section provides the reader with information about the company or with brief details of previous events. This will enable the reader to read the body of your report in the light of this information. Therefore he will understand your report more clearly and so be more likely to accept your conclusions.

What Else Can We Learn from the Japanese?, published by the National Productivity Board of Singapore, considers 10 different Japanese companies. The writers give some background information about each company. e.g.

Komatsu

'Komatsu Limited was established in 1921 to manufacture machine tools and mining equipment. In 1981, the company expanded its production to include farm tractors. Since then, Komatsu Ltd. has developed numerous sophisticated construction equipment. Currently, it has a workforce of 16,700. In 1984, it was ranked no. 2 in the world in the production of construction equipment. Sales in 1985 totalled 576 billion yen. This represented an increase of 13 per cent compared to the previous year. The company was awarded the prestigious Derming prize for its quality control (QC) activities in 1964 and 1981.'

From this background, the reader is immediately aware of the size and fine reputation of this company, especially in the area of quality control. It also justifies the selection of Komatsu for the study on Japanese productivity practices.

In some reports, especially those requiring recommendations, instead of using 'Background' as a sub-heading, the word 'Problem' is used. As a report writer, it is your job to find the best solution to the problem, but it is essential that the reader is clear as to the nature of that problem so that he is more likely to accept your recommendations. In other words, certain background details or explanations have to be given.

The report of Singapore's Property Market Consultative Committee entitled 'Action Plan for the Property Sector' describes the seriousness of the problem of over-supply of properties:

> 'The upshot of the surge in building activities has been an over-supply situation. The situation is likely to persist or even deteriorate in the coming years if the performance of the Singapore economy continues to be weak and nothing is done to redress the woes in the property market.
>
> In practical terms this over-supply spells among other things, a waste of capital tied up in idle assets, a phasing out of jobs in the construction and related sectors ... The problem before us is thus of national significance; it should be worrying not merely to owners of unsold or unoccupied space, but also, directly or indirectly, to the rest of the population.'

5. Definition of terms

If you have any doubts concerning the reader's understanding of a specialised term you are using, you should define or explain it. Should there be a number of such terms, these ought to be included in a glossary at the end of the report, and the introduction should refer the reader to this glossary.

Below are two examples of terms being defined or explained. The first one is a technical report entitled 'CNC retrofitting — from an educational project to its role in the manufacturing industry'.

'CNC retrofitting is a process of adding Computer Numerical Control (CNC) to a machine in order to enhance its performance capability and prolong its useful working life.'

The second example is taken from the report, 'Action Plan for the Property Sector'.

'There is convention or consensus among countries or cities as to what "excessive supply" means. For the purpose of this action plan, an over-supply exists if the occupancy levels are below the healthy norm of, say, 90 per cent for homes and shops, 85 per cent for offices, factories and warehouses, and 70 per cent for hotels.'

6. **Method of investigation**

This could be referred to as 'method of enquiry', 'procedures' or 'sources of information', and includes a statement on **how** you obtained the information that the report contains. Did you conduct a survey? Did you make a study of any particular literature? Did you conduct any experiments or interviews?

Thus, by explaining how, you also mention **where** from, i.e., the sources.

This can be written in a report as:

'The information in this report was gathered from a questionnaire distributed to all the factory workers, from interviews with nine of these employees, including all three supervisors, and during discussions with the company's personnel officers. In order to assess the extent of the problem, use was made of a similar report entitled 'Employee Absenteeism', written in 1983 before the factory moved to its present location.'

Let's see how these aspects of the introduction can be included in actual reports. You will notice that not all reports contain all six aspects. The amount of information to be included in the introduction depends on the writer's assessment of the reader's familiarity with the subject of the report. The less the reader knows, the more the writer must include, yet the introduction should not be excessively long. In fact it should not exceed 1/6 of the total length of the report.

Example: A MARKET RESEARCH REPORT

1. INTRODUCTION

    A. Background and objectives

    > Shok chocolate drink was advertised throughout the Asean region in April/May 1987. A commercial entitled 'Long Distance Sportsman' was aired in the Philippines whilst 'Soccer Special' (which had been used previously) was shown in the other Asean countries. The former commercial is a 30-second version, while 'Soccer Special' is 20 seconds long. [BACKGROUND]
    >
    > The new 'Long Distance Sportsman' commercial was designed to communicate that Shok is a chocolate drink which is:
    >
    > - modern and up-to-date
    > - refreshing
    > - nourishing
    > - better than other chocolate drinks
    >
    > Research was needed to assess the impact and communication of the 'Long Distance Sportsman' commercial and to discover any advantages or disadvantages of moving to it from the 'Soccer Special'. Thus, the main objectives of this report are:
    >
    > i) to determine the strengths and weaknesses of the two commercials in terms of communication and image shifts; [PURPOSE]
    >
    > ii) to determine how persuasive the new 'Long Distance Sportsman' commercial is;
    >
    > iii) to compare the impact of the 'Long Distance Sportsman' and 'Soccer Special' commercials;

RECOMMENDATION | iv) to recommend which (if either) of the two commercials should be used in future advertising campaigns.

SCOPE | An impact and communication check was carried out on an earlier Shok commercial, 'Bedtime Beverage' (September 1984) and, where applicable, comparisons have been made.

METHOD OF INVESTIGATION | **B. Method**

The sample recruited to test the Shok commercials consisted of:

i) those who play a sport regularly, with quota controls on age and sex;

ii) housewives with children aged between 2 and 18.

The respondents were shown a reel of 10 commercials with one of Shok in fifth position.

After seeing the reel, the respondents were asked to recall as many of the advertisements as possible. They were subsequently prompted for recall of Shok if it was not remembered spontaneously and asked what the main thing was that the commercial was communicating.

The test commercial was then shown again on its own and questions covered:

- further communication
- likelihood of buying Shok (plus reasons)
- detailed recall of content of the advertisement
- things found hard to believe/understand
- likes and dislikes about advertisement
- overall opinion of advertisement
- image of Shok from advertisement

- attitudes to Shok and other chocolate drinks
- prompted comments on advertisement
- product usage

Field work was carried out between 20 and 26 September 1987 in each of the Asean countries. In order that comparisons could be made between the different countries, the number of respondents interviewed in each country was identical, namely 50.

Example: AN INFORMATION REPORT

INTRODUCTION   BACKGROUND

Interest in Japanese productivity practices in general, and management practices in particular, has been growing from strength to strength. This is not surprising in view of Japan's sustained economic growth and high standard of living at a time when other industrialised nations seem to be plagued by economic woes. The consensus is that there is much that can be learnt from the Japanese experience.

In Singapore, Japanese productivity practices have been given much publicity as they constituted a significant source of inspiration for launching the Productivity Movement in September 1981. Although it is true that the Productivity Movement here is not modelled strictly or completely after the Japanese experience, many aspects of it bear traces of Japanese influence. Because of the success of Japanese management practices in increasing productivity and business efficiency, many books on them have been published. These publications have played an important role in disseminating useful information to Singapore companies. The proliferation of literature on Japanese management practices makes one wonder what else we can learn from the Japanese. As it turned out, the majority of the books deal with the subject on a general level, glossing over different practices in Japanese companies, and presenting only a broad-brush picture of how the various management practices work. After five years of the Productivity Movement, our understanding of the Japanese management practices has improved. This is a result of study missions to Japan, the attachment of Japanese experts to the National Productivity Board (NPB) and the sending of NPB staff to Japan under the Productivity Development Project (PDP) sponsored by the Japanese government.

METHOD OF ENQUIRY

The training given under the PDP includes company attachment, where participants get the opportunity of gaining first-hand experience of how Japanese companies tick. Thus, they are able to observe how textbook theory is translated into practice at the workplace.

SCOPE

This publication presents case studies of 10 Japanese companies visited by the 3rd batch of PDP fellows in 1985. These 10 companies are:

a) Aisin Seiki
b) Shimizu Food Center
c) Isetan
d) Canon
e) Hokuetsu Paper Mills
f) Yamatake-Honeywell
g) Komatsu (Oyama Plant)
h) Okamoto Machine Tool Works
i) Nippon Kokan
j) Yaohan Department Store

PURPOSE

Companies in Singapore will find the accounts of the management practices in these 10 companies quite an eye-opener. They will be able to get an idea of what else they can learn, other than what is commonly written on Japanese management systems. They can then consider modifying and adapting them for application at their own workplaces.

Example: A FEASIBILITY REPORT

INTRODUCTION | BACKGROUND

As a result of previous national development plans, there has been considerable improvement in agricultural production in the interior of the country, and now national rice production can adequately meet domestic requirements. The success of this project has contributed to the decision of the government to investigate the possibility of developing agriculture in coastal areas.

Subsequently, in March 1986, Technicasia was commissioned by the government to carry out a feasibility study on a coastal agriculture project. In presenting the results of the study, this report assesses the potential of technological modernisation and describes the existing soil conditions in order to determine the possibility of crop diversification. The anticipated benefits resulting from the implementation of this project are also discussed. | PURPOSE

SCOPE

This report is based on the findings of a team of consultants who visited the area from May to September 1986. Data was also collected from discussions with government officials and farmers. In addition, use was made of the reports on the interior agriculture project insofar as they relate to the present study. | METHOD OF ENQUIRY

COMMENTS ON THE THREE INTRODUCTIONS

1. **A market research report**

    This introduction is long because the **method** is described in detail. This is necessary because the reader needs to be certain that the sample is suitable and that the method will ensure reliable results.

    The **objectives** are enumerated so that they are absolutely clear to both reader and writer.

2. An information report

The **purpose** is sometimes not expressed in sufficient depth in an information report since the writer may think he is merely imparting information on a certain topic to the reader. The basic purpose of the above report is to present 'accounts of the management practices in these 10 companies'. However, this purpose is too superficial, and thus the writer suggests how the reader could make use of this information by 'modifying and adapting them (the Japanese management systems) for application at their own workplaces'.

The **scope** is an essential element since the reader needs to know more precisely the areas of information included in the report.

The **background** explains the reasons for the report, namely, the success of Japanese management practices, the interest of Singaporeans in these practices and the lack of literature examining these practices in specific Japanese companies. These reasons justify the writing of the report, contribute an element of persuasion to encourage the reader to read further, and inform the reader what to expect by suggesting that this report contains a deeper examination of Japanese management practices.

The **method of enquiry** explains how the information was obtained — largely by first-hand experience.

3. A feasibility report

The **background** to this report is fairly short as it should be, since writers must be selective in the information they put in the background section. Some writers wish to provide readers with all the information the latter may be interested in knowing, and at the same time they hope to impress readers with the thoroughness of their research. This temptation should be resisted since the reader needs to know only what will help him understand the report more easily.

The distinction between **scope** and **purpose** is not always clear in an introduction which does not have sub-headings. It could be argued that the purposes of this report are

Writing the introduction

(i) to assess the potential of technological modernisation, and

(ii) to describe the existing soil conditions.

However, these two apparent objectives of the report develop from the single purpose of 'presenting the results of the feasibility study to determine the possibility of crop diversification'. Hence, those two aspects make up part of the scope.

You will have noticed that the different elements of the introduction may be stated as a sub-heading or they may be discernible from an unbroken text. A major criterion in deciding whether to use sub-headings is that of length. The longer the introduction, the more likely you will use sub-headings.

Remember though, that the information should not be unnecessarily long. Its main purpose is to enable the reader to understand the body of the report more easily.

6 Using language that communicates

Having planned the body of your report, you now have to express those points in language which will communicate the information effectively to the reader. In order to achieve effective communication your language must be

Correct
Concise
Clear
Cohesive
Objective
Readable
Appropriate

CORRECT

Your English must be correct in four areas:

Diction
Grammar
Spelling
Punctuation

DICTION

Diction is your 'choice of words and phrases' (*Longman*

Dictionary of Contemporary English). In your choice of a particular word you need to consider not only its **denotative** and **connotative** meanings, but also whether it **collocates** with the words next to it.

Denotation

Each word conveys a certain meaning and you must ensure that you have chosen the correct word to reflect your intended meaning. A football report in *The Straits Times* contained this sentence:

'If Wigan reach the semi-finals — and Leeds will be without Brendan Ormsby, Ian Baird and Bobby Macdonald because of suspension and illegibility — it may be high noon for the policemen trying to pacify the 2,000 Leeds fans to be allowed into the 12,500 capacity ground.'

Which is the incorrect word?

Leeds cannot be without certain players due to 'illegibility'. 'Illegibility' means 'inability to be read'. The correct word is 'ineligibility', meaning that the players did not qualify for selection for the match.

The two words 'illegibility' and 'ineligibility' sound and look similar, hence the error. It is important to check that your words have the intended denotation. Appendix 1 gives a list of words that are often used incorrectly.

Connotation

Whereas the denotation of a word is 'the thing pointed to by a word', its connotation is 'a meaning or idea suggested by a word or thing in addition to the formal meaning or nature of the word or thing'. (*Longman Dictionary of Contemporary English*).

This 'meaning or idea suggested' is very important because it generally expresses your attitude. You can, for example, describe a man who refuses to change his mind as either 'determined' (positive connotation), or 'stubborn' (negative).

In a report, the choice of one of these words rather than the other is a clear expression of your attitude, and this in turn is likely to influence the reader.

Adjectives have particularly strong connotations. Consider the following words:

Slim   Slender   Thin   Skinny

'Slim' and 'slender' carry positive connotations, whereas 'thin' is neutral and 'skinny', for most people, is negative.

You cannot, however, ignore cultural differences. 'Plump' may be a compliment in some cultures, but a criticism in others. 'Chubby' can be regarded as the ideal for children, but not for adults.

A more serious example will further illustrate cultural differences. What is the name given to the person who helps to clean your house? In Asian countries, she is sometimes called a servant or maid. If you ever called the Western cleaning lady either of these names (especially the former) she would leave immediately. 'Domestic help' or 'home help' are more positive and polite names.

Connotations also change with history. In the Philippines, the word 'loyalist' to describe a supporter of President Marcos has changed from something of which to be proud to a term of abuse in some circles.

You may have seen the TV series or read the book *'Yes, Minister'*. In one of the stories the conversation went like this. ('I' is the minister.)

> 'Humphrey, are you telling me that BES (British Electronics Systems) got the contract through bribery?' I asked.
>
> He looked pained. 'I wish you wouldn't use words like "bribery", Minister.'
>
> I asked if he'd prefer that I use words like slush fund, sweeteners, or brown envelopes. He patronisingly informed me that these are, in his view, extremely crude and unworthy expressions for what is no more than creative negotiation. 'It is general practice,' he asserted.

The expression 'creative negotiation' carries positive connotations as opposed to the negative ones conveyed by 'bribery', 'slush fund' etc.

Using language that communicates

Using a word which conveys different connotations from what you intended can be more serious than using a word with the wrong denotation, because connotations express attitudes.

Collocation

'Collocation is the way that some words occur regularly whenever another word is used.'
(Collins Cobuild English Language Dictionary.)

        CO   +   LOCATION
      (with)   (place)

Example: Strong   coffee

There are many so-called synonyms for 'strong', such as 'powerful', 'forceful', 'pungent' and 'tough', but none of these collocates with 'coffee'.

'Tough' is used with 'meat', and the opposite is 'tender', not 'soft'. 'Pungent' refers to 'smell', etc.

Check then that the words you have chosen fit the other words in the sentence, i.e. they collocate.

SPELLING

Many engineers find difficulty with spelling, even though they are native speakers of English. In personal letters to friends spelling mistakes do not matter provided they do not impede communication, but in a formal report wrong spelling indicates a lack of thoroughness. You have not taken the trouble to use a dictionary to check your spelling nor have you asked a colleague for help. The reader may well suspect that since you have written the report hastily your research may also lack thoroughness.

You do not want to create a negative attitude on the part of the reader, and so you must take care and time with your spelling. Appendix 2 gives certain spelling rules with a list of commonly misspelt words.

GRAMMAR

As with spelling, grammatical errors are serious only when they impede communication. Similarly incorrect grammar will have a negative effect on the reader who may have doubts about your professionalism. Appendix 3 gives examples of common grammatical errors and explains the rules that need to be followed.

PUNCTUATION

Report writers sometimes concentrate on the words they are using, or the grammar and forget the vital role played by punctuation. Punctuation serves to make your writing absolutely clear to the reader as explained in Appendix 4.

CONCISE

At the planning stage you have omitted all information that is not relevant to the purpose of the report or the reader. Therefore as regards content your report will be concise.

Conciseness, however, applies to language as well as to content. This means that all superfluous words must be omitted. The main sources of superfluous words are **repetition, wordiness,** and **transition sentences.**

Repetition

If there is a particularly important point which you want to emphasise, you may choose to repeat it to ensure that the reader realises its significance. This can be effective provided you do not repeat every point you make, or repeat the same point many times.

Unnecessary repetition

As one of the recommendations of the previous report on lack of punctuality, it was recommended that flexitime be introduced to enable each employee to arrive at work at a time that was suitable for him/her. Following the implementation of the above recommendation, the punctuality of the workers improved initially since they were able to commence work at a time that was convenient to them. However, within three months of the implementation of flexitime, lack of punctuality was as serious a problem as before its introduction.

Using language that communicates

Notice all the repetitions, particularly 'recommendation', 'lack of punctuality', 'able to commence/arrive at work at a time that was suitable to/convenient for them'. In addition, certain unnecessary phrases are included even though the meaning is clear without them, for example, 'of the workers', 'of the implementation of flexitime'. In fact, this paragraph could be shortened by 40 per cent.

Without unnecessary repetition
'The previous report on lack of punctuality recommended the introduction of flexitime to enable each employee to commence work at the most convenient time for him/her. Following the implementation of flexitime, punctuality improved initially, but within three months, the situation was no different from what it had been previously.'

An extract from Action Plan for the Property Sector will illustrate the value of effective repetition.

Effective repetition
The problem before us is thus of national significance; it should be worrying not merely to owners of unsold or unoccupied space but also, directly or indirectly, to the rest of the population. Any non-utilization of available space is a cost to the country. As a corollary, any measure taken to alleviate the problem is for the national good, transcending narrower sectional or parochial interests.

The writer is determined to point out that the problem of over-supply is a matter which affects ALL Singaporeans. He successfully achieves this appropriate emphasis by the repetition of 'nation' and by 'not only owners ... but also the rest of the population'.

Another aspect of repetition to be avoided is **tautology**, which is repeating what one is saying in different words.

The unanimous decision was agreed by every member of the
    committee.

The pipes burst one after another in succession.
It has been proved conclusively, beyond the shadow of a doubt that ...
The piece of equipment is rectangular in shape.

More concise versions would be:

The committee's decision was unanimous. ('Unanimous' means 'agreed by everyone'.)
The pipes burst in succession.
It has been proved ... ('conclusively' is redundant as well as 'beyond the shadow of a doubt' because 'proved' indicates that there is definite evidence. Therefore 'conclusively' serves merely to emphasise 'proved'.)
The piece of equipment is rectangular.

Wordiness

Report writers often believe that if they add some **impressive looking words** it will make their report more acceptable to the reader. Very often these words are superfluous. For example, the conclusion to a report about a new site for an engineering factory stated

The site exhibits satisfactory characteristics for the implementation of the company's construction programme.

What does 'The site exhibits satisfactory characteristics' mean? It simply means 'The site is suitable'.
What is 'the company's construction programme' that is going to be implemented? It is the building of the new engineering factory. Therefore a more concise conclusion would be

The site is suitable for the building of the new engineering factory.

Not only is this sentence more concise but it is also more precise in that it states what the construction programme is, and is therefore clearer.

Using language that communicates

Report writers must resist the temptation to add **words which do not contribute to the meaning.**

It is essential that changes in the level of temperature should be avoided at all costs.

'Level' contributes nothing to the meaning and so should be omitted, while 'essential' and 'at all costs' serve the same purpose of stressing the importance of the avoidance of temperature changes. By replacing 'should' with the stronger 'must' this importance can be retained. Thus the sentence could be shortened without affecting the meaning.

Temperature changes must be avoided.

This tendency of report writers to be verbose is illustrated by the high number of **circumlocutions** to be found in reports. A circumlocution is 'a way of saying something that is longer than necessary' (*Longman Dictionary of Contemporary English*). The following list contains examples of common circumlocutions and more concise expressions.

CIRCUMLOCUTION	CONCISE VERSION
in close proximity to	near / close to
at this point in time	now
arrived at a decision to	decided to
in view of the foregoing circumstances	therefore
a greater number of	more
a sufficient number of / an adequate number of	enough
on account of the fact that	because
in spite of the fact that	although
in the event that	if
in the majority of instances	generally

Transition sentences

It has already been mentioned (on Page 45) that there is no need to write transition sentences to indicate the end of one section of a report and the start of a new section. A typical transition sentence is:

'Those are the advantages of locating the new factory on Site A. Now let us turn our attention to the disadvantages.'

Headings and subheadings inform the reader of the end of one section and the start of a new one, and so transition sentences must be omitted.

As a form of transition sentence report writers sometimes like to write an introductory phrase or sentence at the beginning of a section. A typical introductory sentence to a conclusion is:

'Taking into account all the various aspects of the problem that have been discussed above, it is now possible to reach a satisfactory conclusion.'

Of course a conclusion is based on the information presented in the body of the report, and so the above sentence is unnecessary. Present the facts in the body and your conclusion without a long preamble.

CLEAR

Clarity is the most vital aspect of style in report writing. The report may contain grammatical errors and be verbose, but so long as the reader can understand the meaning the report is acceptable. If he misunderstands what you have written he may make a wrong decision for which you will be responsible. When a report is clear the reader will not have to spend time deciphering what you have written, and so clarity is also a time saver.

Since clarity is so important, we must consider the question 'How can I make my report clear?'

Familiar words

The tendency to use what are believed to be impressive words is far too prevalent in reports. One journalist recently commented that fine sounding words give the false impression that your report is extremely important and that appropriate action is being taken to ensure that all problems are resolved. His article was entitled 'Words Speak Louder ...' (i.e. the words sound more impressive than the action that is actually going to be taken.)

Here is an example from an evaluation report:

> 'Inadequate data on system parameters and benefits is a critical impediment to performance. Reliable assessment of the project's impact remains unattainable. The potential benefits of the project facilities may be dissipated by inadequate attention to crop husbandry and irrigation management.'

This may sound impressive, but the writer is really saying 'I couldn't get enough information and so I can't comment'.

Do not try to impress the reader by using long words which you have found in a thesaurus or dictionary and the meaning of which you are not absolutely certain. Think of the reader too who may not be familiar with such words. It is better to use words which you and the reader know, and to express your thoughts or information simply and clearly.

Watch your jargon

Webster's New Collegiate Dictionary provides the following two definitions of jargon:

1. The **technical terminology** or characteristic idiom of a special activity or group.
2. **Obscure and often pretentious language** marked by circumlocutions and long words.

Technical terminology

This definition of 'jargon' indicates that a particular group has its own terminology. Thus there is legal jargon, engineering jargon, computer jargon etc. Here is an example of economics jargon.

'The economic analysis of the proposed project is based on the financial analysis appropriately adjusted for transfer payments and international prices to reflect export parity price.'

Some knowledge of economics is necessary to understand what the writer is saying.
Should such jargon be used in reports?
The answer is dependent on the answers to two further questions.

a. Who is the intended reader?
b. Will he understand the terminology I have used?

If the intended reader will understand specialised jargon, then use it, since this is the clearest and most concise means of expressing your thoughts. However, if he is not an expert on that subject, you should use layman's language, meaning that you should choose words which can be understood by those who are not trained in that particular field.

Occasionally, you will have to employ a technical word because there is no suitable alternative, but this should be explained, as 'layman's language' has been in the last paragraph, or a glossary could be provided. Similarly, for the first mention of abbreviations or acronyms, they should be stated in full, with the initials in parentheses.

'The two alternatives to the computerised Kriging method of computing ore reserves are the zonal approach (ZA) and the conventional inverse distance squared method (CIDS).'

Obscure language

The negative connotations of 'jargon' are based on this second definition. Writers use pretentious language either because they believe that by so doing they will impress their superiors, or perhaps because they are trying to cover up the lack of substance in what they are writing.

Apart from long, often unfamiliar words, and circumlocutions, a predominant feature of this pretentious style is long noun phrases.

'A fruit and vegetable export marketing study.'
'The country's rich natural resource endowment.'

Using language that communicates

These noun phrases can be made clearer by

i. the use of prepositions to break the long noun phrase into shorter noun phrases.

'A study on the marketing of fruit and vegetable exports.'

ii. the omission of unnecessary words to shorten the noun phrase.

'The country's rich natural resources.'

When a writer employs technical terminology and obscure language, the reader will have great difficulty in understanding.

Not surprisingly, a journalist criticised a commentary sent to investors wanting advice on where to put their money in the coming year. This commentary contained expressions such as:

'tightened resource utilisation', 'global portfolio strategies', 'ongoing net requirement of equities outstanding', and 'a shift towards a more defensive investment posture will be warranted'.

I doubt whether the small investor would be any the wiser after reading these expressions. It is essential therefore, that writers avoid the use of jargon in the sense of 'obscure, pretentious language', and employ technical terminology only when they believe it can be understood by the intended reader.

Concrete words

A concrete word describes something you can see, touch or smell. The opposite of 'concrete' is 'abstract', and it is difficult sometimes to perceive abstract words with one's imagination.

Concrete	Abstract
Machine	Truth
House	Friendship
Factory	Many words ending in -tion or -ness e.g. presumption; awareness

A report may conclude:

> 'Awareness of the location of fire extinguishers is a vital aspect of safety officers' responsibilities.'

This would be much clearer and more concise if the abstract 'awareness' were avoided.

> 'Safety officers must know the location of fire extinguishers.'

Using concrete words also makes the report more interesting to the reader and as a result he will not only be more likely to read the whole report, but also consider it more favourably.

Precise words

Concrete words tend to be more precise than abstract ones, but the need for precision must be explained further. When a report contains generalisations it may often be the result of inadequate research.

> 'The machine breaks down frequently.'

The reader wants to know 'How frequently?' If you do not say he will assume you do not know.

The following recommendation is clearly absurdly vague.

> 'It appears that some of the machinery could be replaced in the not too distant future.'

The writer has no confidence in this recommendation, otherwise he would write 'should' rather than 'could' and would have omitted 'it appears that'. Words such as 'seem', 'appear', 'think', 'might', 'could' indicate doubt in the mind of the writer. He needs to be sure of his facts and believe that his conclusions and recommendations are logical and appropriate. Further vagueness is shown in 'the not too distant future'.

Being precise and specific adds to the clarity of your report and at the same time provides evidence of thorough research and clear thinking.

Active rather than passive

PASSIVE: From the tests that have been conducted in the workshop it has been proved that the machine is not faulty.

ACTIVE: The tests conducted in the workshop prove that the machine is not faulty.

The active is more direct and concise, and places the emphasis on the subject of the action. Thus in the above example the active makes it much clearer that the subject of 'prove' is 'tests'. The active makes the report more interesting to read because of its directness and reference to the subject.

In the passive the emphasis is on the action, and the subject is often omitted. Thus 'tests' could be omitted — 'It has been proved that ...'. This, however can lead to vague, imprecise writing. On the other hand, the inclusion of the subject, usually preceded by the word 'by' or 'from' in the above example, makes your writing long-winded. Therefore the active is normally preferable to the passive.

There are, however, two uses of the passive.

1. **When the subject of the action is not important.**

    The report entitled 'Photography for Drawings' (see Chapter 12) states that

    'The photographs can be enlarged on our photocopiers to the required size for drawings.'

    It is not important who will enlarge the photographs and so the passive is used, thereby placing appropriate emphasis on the action.
    Similarly a description of a process is written in the passive.

    PASSIVE: 'The trunks are transported to the paper mill and placed in the shredder.'

    Who carried out the action? The workers.

ACTIVE: 'The workers transported the trunks to the paper mill and placed them in the shredder.'

Clearly 'the workers' is an unimportant subject which takes the focus away from the action. Thus the passive is better.

2. **When the subject of the action is not known or best kept secret.**

    'Various decisions regarding the premises will need to be taken concerning the standard of sound proofing, air conditioning, lighting and so forth.'

It is not known exactly who will take the decisions, hence the passive.

The passive may be used to avoid direct criticism of any one individual.

    'The recommendations made at the last board meeting have not yet been implemented.'

Generally, though, the active will be used since not stating the subject may be regarded as a lack of thoroughness in your research. Furthermore, the active is more concise and direct, making your report considerably more readable.

Avoid ambiguity

1. **Pronouns must refer to one and only one noun.**

    'When Mr. Lim reported the matter to the supervisor he told him he would take action.'

To whom does 'he' refer? It could be either Mr. Lim or the supervisor. The ambiguity can be removed by the repetition of the noun; or the use of 'the former' or 'the latter'.

    'When Mr. Lim reported the matter to the supervisor, the latter said he would take action.'

The relative pronoun 'who', 'which', etc. should normally refer to the noun immediately before it.

> 'The refuse at an incineration plant is dropped into the feed hopper which passes down the chute on to the rocking grate.'

Grammatically, 'which' refers to 'feed hopper' but that cannot be the intended meaning. It must be the refuse, not the feed hopper that passes down the chute. The sentence should read

> 'The refuse at an incineration plant is dropped into the feed hopper *and* passes down the chute...'

or

> 'At an incineration plant the refuse which is dropped into the feed hopper passes down the chute...'

2. Position words and phrases correctly.

'Only', a word that is frequently misplaced should normally be put directly before the word to which it refers.

> 'This report only provides information on the factory workers.'

Here 'only' qualifies 'provides', implying that the report does not analyse the information or draw conclusions from it; it only provides the information. This is an unlikely meaning. 'Only' should qualify 'factory workers', which are the only group being considered, not the clerical staff.

> 'This report provides information on only the factory workers.'

Phrases are sometimes misplaced too.

> 'By working an additional shift 10,000 parts were produced for the customer on the production line in 24 hours.'

The customer appears to be 'on the production line'! Correct placement of 'for the customer' would remove the ambiguity.

'... produced on the production line for the customer.'

The longer the sentence, the more likely it is that phrases will be positioned incorrectly. This is particularly true when dates are given.

'A team of consultants was fielded to review available data and recommend the remedial measures to be implemented on site from 18-22 March 1988.'

'The remedial measures' were not supposed to be implemented 'on site from 18-22 March 1988'. This refers to the fielding of the consultants.

'A team of consultants was fielded on site from 18-22 March 1988 to review available data and recommend the remedial measures to be implemented.'

3. **Double negatives are to be avoided.**

They can cause the reader to re-read the sentence because the meaning is not clear.

'It is not impossible that the machine will not be repaired by the end of the month.'

What does this mean? 'Not impossible' indicates that it is 'possible but not very likely', and so 'might' would be a clearer and more concise alternative.

'The machine might not be repaired by the end of the month.'

4. **Parallel constructions.**

Which of the following sentences do you prefer?

    a.   'Productivity can be increased by providing training for

Using language that communicates

the workers, if there is an incentive scheme for them and when the machinery is modernised.'

b.   'Productivity can be increased by providing training for the workers, implementing an incentive scheme for them, and by modernising the machinery.'

Sentence (b) is clearer because it contains parallel constructions. This means that the three related parts of the sentence — 'providing', 'implementing' and 'modernising' are in the same grammatical form. All three end in -ing and refer to the preposition 'by'.

The parallel constructions enable the reader to notice more quickly how many sentence elements are related.

Another example:

'Recession has resulted in retrenchments and the workers being paid less.'

Parallel:

'Recession has resulted in retrenchments and lower wages for the workers.'

Sometimes in reports, lists have to be made. It is then essential that the sentence that introduces the list fits grammatically with each item in the list. In addition, it is preferable if the structure of each item is similar.

'In the feasibility study, special attention will be given to:
i)   development of groundwater resources;
ii) possible participation of the private sector;
iii) development of appropriate water management techniques; and
iv) development of viable water users associations and operation and maintenance services.'

The structure of each item in the above list is similar.

NOUN   +   OF   +   NOUN PHRASE

In addition, each item fits grammatically with the introductory clause 'special attention will be given to ...'

Short sentences

The longer the sentence the more difficult it is to write without making grammatical mistakes or obscuring the meaning. Also the reader will find a long sentence more difficult to understand, and will probably have to read it more than once, thereby wasting time.

> 'Ocean dumping of toxic wastes must be considered not only in the context of the legal constraints imposed by the Oslo Convention of 1972, but also, in view of the growing ecological lobby worldwide, the use of marine eco-systems for recycling, the retention of harmful wastes in the bottom sediments, and the general effects of persistent bio-accumulable substances must be subjected to essential research procedures before we can recommend ocean dumping as a viable alternative to continued use of coastal zones and inland sites.'

Re-writing this sentence in three shorter sentences clarifies the meaning.

> 'Before we can recommend the dumping of toxic wastes in the ocean — rather than continuing to use the coast or inland sites— we must consider the legal and ecological problems. We should research the use of marine eco-systems for recycling, the retention of harmful wastes in sediment, and the effects of bio-accumulable substances. Not only is there a growing ecological lobby worldwide, but also the Oslo Convention of 1972 imposes restrictions on dumping.'

COHESIVE

Cohesive means 'tending to stick together'. In other words, there must be links between sentences, paragraphs, sub-sections, and sections of the report, so that the reader can clearly follow the presentation of facts to reach the same conclusion as the writer.

Planning the report to ensure cohesiveness has been discussed in

Using language that communicates

detail in Chapter 4. It is now necessary to consider how to write cohesive sub-sections and paragraphs.

Unity

All the information in a sub-section should relate directly to that particular topic. The tendency is to add an extra sentence which does not appear to fit anywhere else. If the information in that sentence is important, then another sub-section is necessary, but if it is unimportant, it can be omitted.

Read the paragraph below and decide which sentence does not fit into this paragraph sub-section entitled 'Beneficiaries'.

Beneficiaries

A total of 5,000 farm families, most of whom are small subsistence farmers cultivating less than one hectare will share the direct benefits of the project. The direct beneficiaries of: (i) subsistence rice and vegetable growers (2,600 farms) benefiting from the irrigation component; and (ii) rain-fed vegetable growers (2,400 farms) directly supported under the seed production and marketing components of the project. The annual incremental production of vegetables and rice at full development in 1990 is estimated at about 40,000 mt and 5,000 mt respectively. The project will also indirectly benefit about 300 traders.

The sentence which does not fit is 'The annual incremental production ... respectively.' This sentence describes the **benefits**, not the beneficiaries. Therefore, this information should be included in a different sub-section.

Controlling idea

The golden rule is 'one main idea per paragraph'. When a paragraph contains more than one main idea, it is likely that the report reader, who is skimming through the report for the main ideas, will miss something of importance. In other words, short paragraphs are a sign of clear thinking and an aid to quick understanding.

Topic sentence

The controlling idea is contained in one sentence within the paragraph. This sentence is known as the 'topic sentence'. The remainder of the paragraph should expand upon the topic sentence, giving additional details, examples, explanations etc.

Sometimes the topic sentence comes at the end of the paragraph as a conclusion based on the information given. Alternatively, the topic sentence could be the first sentence of the paragraph. If it is located elsewhere, it will be more difficult for the reader to find. In a report, however, the best location is the first sentence since the report reader who wants to know only the main ideas can find each topic sentence very quickly.

Read the following paragraph taken from the report of the Property Market Consultative Committee's Action Plan for the Property Sector, and locate the topic sentence.

> A conceivable solution to the oversupply problem is to convert existing properties or wherever feasible, plans of potential supply, into alternative uses. In this connection, we note with interest, that apparently on account of the ingenuity of owners, some conversions have been effected. For example, shop space has been converted into eating places; and office space into staff recreational facilities. Such conversions have, however, been on a very modest scale.

The topic sentence is the first sentence with the rest of the paragraph expanding on the proposed solution to the over-supply situation.

Linking words

Using linking words, sometimes called connectives, to show how one sentence or paragraph is related to the previous one is essential to cohesive writing. A list of the most important linking words and their function will provide a useful reference in ensuring that reports are cohesive.

Using language that communicates

Function	Linking Words
1 Introducing a contrast.	But; however; nevertheless; on the other hand; although; in spite of; whereas; while.
2 Adding extra information.	Moreover; furthermore; besides; not only ... but also; in addition.
3 Indicating sequence or listing information.	First(ly); second(ly); then; next; after that; finally; lastly; in the first place.
4 Introducing examples.	For example; such as; for instance; to illustrate.
5 Introducing a result.	As a result; as a consequence; consequently; therefore; hence; thus; so.
6 Introducing a cause.	Because; since; as.
7 Introducing a condition.	If; provided; providing; so long as; unless.
8 Introducing purpose.	In order to; so as to; so that; to.
9 Introducing a comparison.	Similarly; in the same way; likewise.
10 Introducing a summary.	To summarise; to sum up; to conclude; in conclusion; in short.

Read the extract below from a paper entitled Foreign Direct Investment and Economic Growth in the Asian and Pacific Region. The linking words which are highlighted enable the reader to follow the writer's arguments without too much difficulty.

Two	– guides the reader so that he knows what to expect
First	– here is the first reason
Several	– prepares the reader for what is to come
While	– indicates a contrast between foreign direct investment and borrowing from commercial banks
Moreover	– this is the second financial advantage
While	– contrast
In addition	– third financial advantage
in contrast to	– contrast!

Finally	– fourth and last financial advantage
thus	– introduces the consequential benefit
second	– the second basic reason for the renewed interest in the flow of foreign direct investment
Moreover	– additional information to support the second reason
Thus	– introduces a concluding statement for the second reason

Note also that each paragraph contains one main idea and that this topic sentence is at the beginning of the paragraph.

Foreign Direct Investment and Economic Growth in the Asian and Pacific Region

In recent years, there has been a renewed interest in the flow of foreign direct investment to developing countries, both as a source of foreign capital and of improved technology and management systems. The developing (host) and industrial (source) countries, as well as international organizations, increasingly advocate a substantial expansion in the share of foreign direct investment in the overall flow of financial resources to developing countries that have deficits in their balance of payments. Two basic reasons have been suggested for this renewed interest.

First, it is postulated that foreign direct investment has several financial advantages over borrowing from commercial banks. Equity financing requires payments to be made only when the investment earns a profit, while debt requires payments irrespective of the prevailing economic situation. Moreover, payments under foreign direct investment can be regulated by the host country while debt payments are outside its control because of interest rates in international markets. In addition, only a portion of foreign direct investment is typically repatriated in contrast to the need to repay the full amount of principal on loans. Finally, foreign direct investment permits a closer match between the maturity structure of earnings from an investment and that of required payments to the capital used in financing, thus avoiding difficulties when developing countries undertake short-term borrowing to finance long-term investment.

Second, current projections about future official flows, especially official development assistance (ODA), and commercial bank borrowing are less promising than in previous years, and it has been suggested that foreign direct investment can be a useful alternative. ODA from the Development Assistance Committee (DAC) countries of the Organisation for Economic Co-operation and Development (OECD) is expected to increase by only 2 per cent per year in real terms during the next several years. Moreover, lending by commercial banks has been declining since 1982. Thus, there appears to be a reasonable scope for additional foreign direct investment flows to developing countries.

Using language that communicates

Main idea: Renewed interest in the flow of foreign direct investment to developing countries.

Two reasons:

1. Foreign direct investment has several financial advantages over borrowing from commercial banks.

Foreign direct investment	**Borrowing from commercial banks**
	While
a) payments made only when investment earns a profit	payments made irrespective of economic situation
Moreover	**While**
b) payments can be regulated by host country	payments regulated by international interest rates
In addition	**In contrast to**
c) only a portion is typically repatriated	the full amount of principal needs to be repaid
Finally	
d) closer match is possible between maturity structure of earnings and that of required payments	the match is not so close
Thus (consequence) difficulties are avoided regarding short-term borrowing to finance long-term investment	

2. Foreign direct investment can be an alternative since ODA and commercial bank borrowing is not expected to be as high as in the past.

   a) ODA to increase by only 2 per cent

Moreover   b) lending by commercial banks has been declining

Thus   There is scope for additional foreign direct invest-
(conclusion)   ment

Cohesive writing is not only a sign of clear and logical thinking, it is also an invaluable guide to the reader who is trying to locate your main ideas and determine how those ideas are inter-related.

OBJECTIVE

'I' and 'we'

The uses of the active and passive have already been discussed, but linked to this is the use of 'I' and 'we'. Which is better, I/we with the active, or the passive?

> PASSIVE: 'Inspection of the site has been carried out and the following conclusions have been reached.'
>
> ACTIVE: 'We have inspected the site and reached the following conclusions.'

The active is more direct and concise, stating also that the writers themselves carried out the inspection. Therefore the use of 'we' with the active is often preferable to the passive.

Nevertheless, over-use of 'I' and 'we' should be avoided since the emphasis must be on the facts contained in the report. When 'I' and 'we' are used frequently the reader may have the impression that the report is based on the writer's opinions, in other words the report is subjective, whereas it should be objective.

The recommendations can start:

> ACTIVE: I/we recommend that ...
> PASSIVE: It is recommended that ...

Most report writers prefer 'It is recommended that ...' but the active equivalent is quite acceptable, especially if a less formal style is adopted.

Diction

Another aspect of objectivity lies in your choice of words. Since your attitude is conveyed by the connotations (see Page 71) as well as by the denotation of a word, great care needs to be taken to ensure that you have selected neutral words. Any positive or negative words in the findings may suggest to the reader that you are biased.

Adjectives and adverbs are frequently subjective and so beware of the following kinds of expressions:

Dismal failure	– omit 'dismal' because it is purely subjective.
Appalling conditions	– the conditions must be described first before saying they were appalling.
Huge profit	– state the amount of profit. What is huge to the writer may not be huge to the reader.
Only $10,000	– 'only' implies cheapness, which is a subjective value judgement.
Poor quality	– make sure you have proved that the quality is poor.

There is a place for your opinions in an objective report, but that place is in the conclusions, and your opinions must be based on an analysis of the facts that you have presented. Nevertheless, emotive words such as 'dismal' and 'appalling' should generally still be avoided, and exact figures should be given rather than 'huge, cheap'. In other words, be precise and objective instead of vague and subjective.

READABLE

If a report is readable, it means that it can be understood at the first reading, and so it must exhibit the principles of clarity that have been mentioned such as familiar words, no ambiguity, use of the active rather than the passive, and sentences that are not too long.

In addition, application of the following suggestions will increase readability.

Action words

i) Verbs are more forceful than nouns.

    discuss   discussion
    explain   explanation
    calculate   calculation
    install   installation

NOUN: *Installation* of the system took place at the end of May.
VERB: The system was *installed* at the end of May.

Not only does the verb 'installed' lead to a more forceful sentence, it also shortens the sentence because the noun form often requires the addition of a verb.

    discuss   have a discussion
    explain   give an explanation
    calculate   make a calculation

ii) Verbs that are specific are easier to visualise.

    General   **Specific**
    destroy   crush
                        burn
                        explode

The following illustrates five ways in which a sentence can be written illustrating the principle of action verbs and the preference of the active to the passive.

BEST   The manager outlined the policy.
                The manager described the policy.
                The policy was described by the manager.
                The manager gave a description of the policy.
WORST   A description of the policy was given by the manager.

Variety in sentence length

Although short sentences are preferable to long ones, this does not mean that every sentence should be a short simple sentence since this would result in an extremely monotonous style of writing. Instead, the length of sentences should vary since variety enhances the readability of your report.

Visuals

A report which contains tables, graphs etc. to present statistics is more readable than one which records all the statistical information in the form of a long paragraph.

See Chapter 7 for a more detailed consideration of visuals.

APPROPRIATE

The word 'style' has hardly been used in this chapter, yet many report writers are concerned that they should adopt an appropriate style.

What is an appropriate style?

An appropriate style incorporates all the above principles concerning correctness, clarity, conciseness, cohesiveness, objectivity and readability. In addition, reports should be written in a formal style, as opposed to memos and letters which vary in their degree of formality according to the circumstances and the reader.

What is a formal style?

The choice of impressive words, fairly long sentences and the avoidance of 'I' and 'we' are typical of a very formal style. This is not recommended when it adversely affects the clarity of your writing.

Compare the following sentences:

1. I also learnt a lot of information from the long chats I had with some of our factory workers.

2. Considerable information was also obtained from interviews I conducted with several of our factory workers.

3. Interviews were conducted with certain workshop floor operative personnel in order to obtain the required information.

Clearly sentence 3 is the most formal since 'I' has been omitted. We have already discussed the use of 'I' and the active as an alternative to the passive, and concluded that clarity and conciseness are the two major criteria in choosing between them. In other words, the most formal style is not necessarily the best, since as in sentence 3 it is often the least concise and clear. Why not say 'factory workers' rather than 'workshop floor operative personnel'?

Sentence 1 is most informal, not only because of an over-use of the active and 'I' but also due to the choice of words. 'A lot' and 'chats' are expressions that are acceptable in informal memos and everyday conversation, but in an extended report one should use more formal, yet familiar words. Alternatives to 'chats' are 'interviews', 'discussions' or 'conversations', as appropriate, while 'a lot' can be substituted with 'considerable', 'much' or 'further'.

It should be apparent then, that sentence 2 illustrates a clear, fairly concise style which is sufficiently formal for extended reports. However, this sentence could be shortened by removing the unnecessary 'I conducted' and 'of our'.

'Considerable information was also obtained from interviews with several factory workers.'

As you proofread your report, always look for ways to improve it in terms of diction, clarity and conciseness.

SUMMARY

A report may be well researched, well planned and well presented in terms of visual impact, but for a report to communicate effectively, it must also be well written in terms of language use. To be well written the language must be:

Correct

Correctness applies to diction, spelling, grammar and punctuation. With regard to diction, each word you decide to use must not only have the correct denotation but also the correct connotations and collocations.

Concise

The amount of information to be included in the report has been limited by applying the criterion of relevance. The language you use must also be concise.

To ensure conciseness of expression you must avoid unnecessary repetition, wordiness caused by the addition of superfluous words and by circumlocutions, and transition sentences.

Clear

With regard to the language and visual presentation of a report, clarity is the most important quality. The reader will understand your report more easily if you choose familiar, concrete and precise words, making sure that there is no ambiguity in what you have written. In addition you should think of the reader in the extent to which you use jargon.

Clarity is also enhanced by the use of the active voice in preference to the passive, and of parallel constructions where appropriate. Short sentences will also communicate the information more effectively, whilst reducing the possibility of grammatical errors.

Cohesive

Linking words such as 'thereby', 'such as' and 'since', are essential to guide the reader through your report, pointing out to him the relationship in terms of meaning between one sentence or one paragraph and the next. The report then becomes cohesive, exhibiting a logical development of thought.

Objective

A report should contain facts, not opinions because it must be objective in the information it presents. In addition the words used to communicate that information must be neutral since the connotations of certain words can convey subjective attitudes, often involving criticism.

Readable

Make sure that your report is not only easily understood, but also interesting to read by using verbs, especially ones that create a visual impact. Variety in sentence length and the use of visuals will also add to your report's readability.

Appropriate

An appropriate style for reports is a formal style, but do not employ an overly formal style which adversely affects clarity, conciseness and readability.

7 Making a visual impact

In a report you communicate facts to the reader. We tend to assume that communication means using words, forgetting that non-verbal means of communication can be more effective. By non-verbal, I mean 'not using words'. Here is a list of some common means of non-verbal communication.

Written

Illustrations
Signs
Colour e.g. red for danger
Shape e.g. Highway Code signs
Size (the larger the more important) e.g. capital letters
Emboldening and underlining (to indicate importance)

Non-written

Loudness and tone of voice
Signals
Gestures
Facial expressions
Body language

Non-verbal means of communication are often more powerful than the verbal, often betraying the truth that words try to disguise. When you tell an anecdote at a party someone may comment 'How interesting!', but at the same time he stifles a yawn, looks over your shoulder and winks at a friend. You immediately realise that he was not in the least interested in what you had to say.

Since words are not always the best way of communicating information you must use all possible means at your disposal to present the information as clearly, interestingly and concisely as possible. The non-verbal means of enhancing **written** communication can be divided into **layout** and **illustrations**.

LAYOUT

Why is layout important?

Because a clearly presented report provides the following benefits:

1. **It increases readability.**

    The reader is a busy man who wants to read the report as quickly and effortlessly as possible. He may only want to pick out specific information. A clear layout will enable him to do this.

2. **It aids memory.**

    With a numbering system and headings, the main points contained in a report and the section where they are located can be more easily remembered.

3. **It conveys the right impression about the writer.**

    A clear layout indicates that the writer is a clear thinker and has taken the trouble to present his report to the reader in such a way that the latter will have as little difficulty as possible in understanding it.

4. **It develops a positive attitude in the reader.**

    This follows on from conveying the right impression. Once the reader has a positive attitude you have a greater chance of persuading him to accept your recommendations.

5. **It results in effective communication.**

Your goal is effective communication and layout is as important in achieving this as a logical plan and clear language.

How can I ensure that the layout results in more effective communication?

There are several ways of doing this:

- Paragraphing
- Spacing
- Headings
- Numbering system
- Capitals
- Underlining
- Emboldening

Paragraphing. It has already been mentioned in Chapter 6 that paragraphs should be short, containing one main idea or piece of information with additional details to support or expand on it. Using paragraphs in this way makes your communication much clearer to the reader since he is not confused by a mass of information which he has to unravel in order to pick out the main points. Thus the immediate impression conveyed by a report is partially attributable to the use of paragraphs. If a page contains only one or two long paragraphs the reader may feel less kindly disposed towards the content, knowing that the writer has made his task difficult.

Spacing. It follows then, that the reader likes to see plenty of white space on the page. You should leave a couple of lines between paragraphs and more between sections.

Headings. These have been discussed at length in Chapter 4, but it must be stressed that they are vital in guiding the reader through your report so that he knows the topic of each section.

Numbering system. Headings alone may be sufficient for short reports, but in long ones a numbering system shows the relationship between headings and sub-headings, and it facilitates easy reference to a particular section. Further details concerning the use of a numbering system are given in Chapter 4.

Capitals/underlining/emboldening. These are techniques of highlighting headings, sub-headings and other key words or phrases. Headings are frequently written in capitals and sometimes underlined too, while the sub-headings are printed in lower case letters and underlined. The headings in the report outlined in Fig. 4.2 are to be found in the report itself as:

    2.   ORGANISATION
          2.1   Legal-Entity

          2.2   Governing-Body

               ----

    3.   FINANCE
          3.1   Funding

          3.2   Costs

ILLUSTRATIONS

What purpose do illustrations serve?

1.   **They present information in a more digestible form.**

      The reader needs to be able to understand the information in the report and mull it over in his mind as he reads. This is not possible when a mass of statistical information is presented in the form of connected paragraphs because he has to digest the figures first.

Making a visual impact

This is illustrated in the following paragraph about water supply coverage in a developing country.

'National water supply coverage for 1988 is estimated at 52%, made up of 75% of the urban population and 39% of the rural population. This is a marked improvement on the national figure of 38% in 1984, which included 63% of the urban population and 23% of the rural population. It is expected, however, that with the implementation of the Government's Five-Year Plan, coverage by 1993 will be extended to 95% of the urban population and 63% of the rural population, with overall coverage of 74%.'

The repetition of words and the mass of statistics make the above paragraph indigestible. It would have been much easier for the reader to digest the information if it had been presented in tabular form as in Figure 7.1.

WATER SUPPLY COVERAGE (%)

	NATIONAL	URBAN	RURAL
1984	38	63	23
1988	52	75	39
1993	74	95	63

Fig. 7.1 Table presenting statistical information in a digestible form

2. **They accelerate the speed of understanding.**

   Illustrations enable the reader to understand the information not just at the first reading but even at a glance. This is especially true of pie charts which show percentages, and bar charts and graphs that quickly indicate rises or falls.

3. **They add clarity and precision.**

   A description of a piece of equipment can never be as clear to the reader as an accurate drawing.

4. **They create a visual impact.**

   We tend to remember more easily and in more detail what we have seen rather than what we have read. Illustrations can therefore be very effective in making an impact on the reader, provided they are good illustrations.

What is a good illustration?

A good illustration is one that is:

Relevant. An attractive illustration may have a certain visual appeal, but the reader must see how it is relevant to the purpose of the report.

Identified. Each illustration must have a caption indicating the topic of the information it is providing.

Integrated. The illustration must be related to the section of the report in which it is located. The text must refer to the illustration, pick out significant details and provide any necessary explanations.

Meaningful. The illustration must tell the reader what you want him to know. This may mean choosing between different types of illustration. A graph shows trends whereas a table gives precise figures. You must decide which one is going to be more meaningful in relation to your particular report.

Clear. Of course illustrations must be presented attractively and neatly, but by 'clear' I mean more than that. It is possible to mislead the reader who merely skims through your report by presenting your illustrations so that they reinforce your point of view. Two techniques are shown on the following page:

Making a visual impact

i) Adjusting the horizontal axis.

**Taiwan's growth in labour cost (per worker) 1976-1983
(base year 1975)**

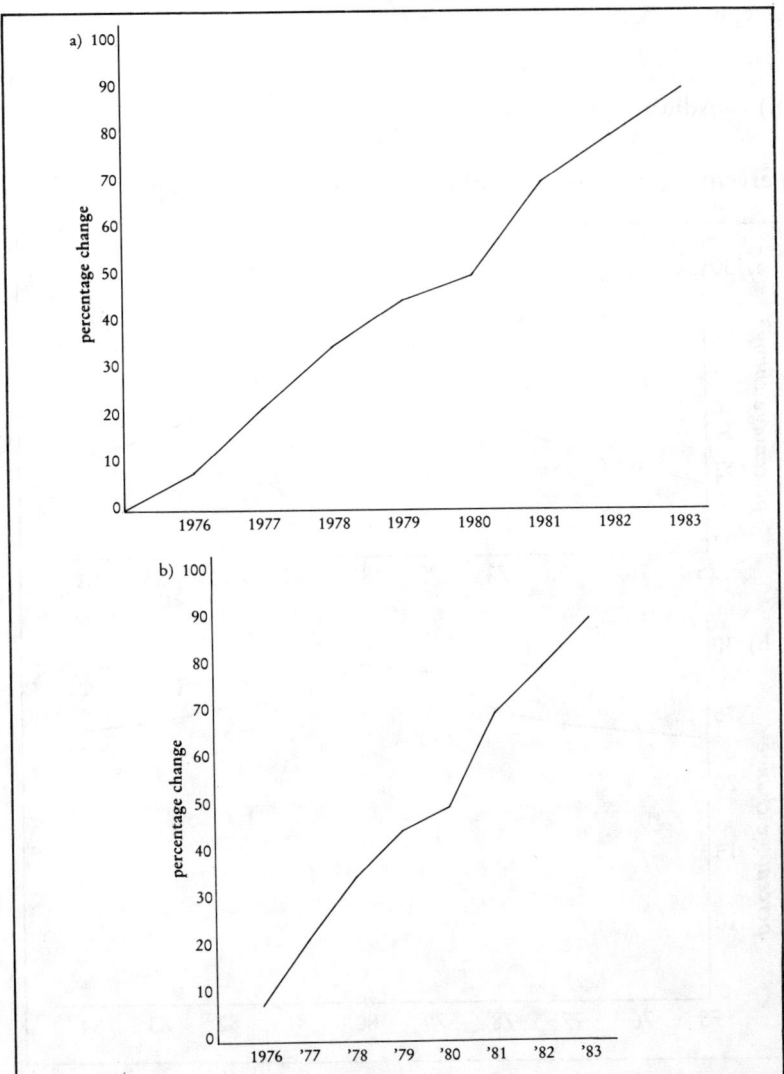

Fig 7.2 Adjusting the horizontal axis gives a graph a different appearance.

It appears that the first graph indicates a much slower increase in wages than the second one because the line rises more slowly. On closer examination you will see that both graphs provide the same information. By shortening the horizontal axis the line rises more steeply.

ii) Adjusting the scale.

Percentage contribution of manufacturing to Singapore's GDP

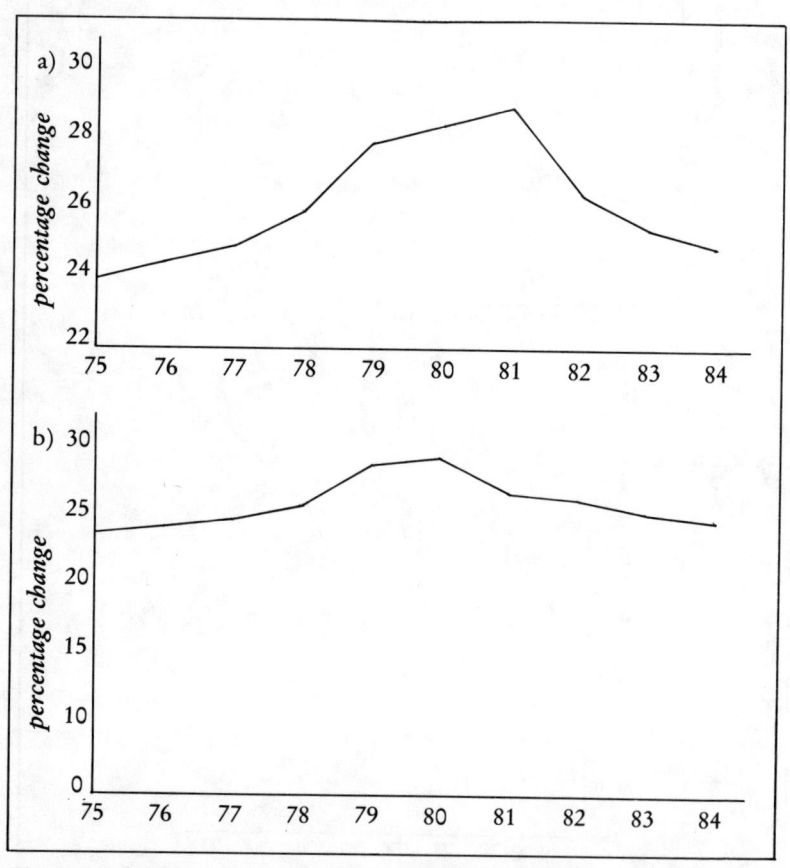

Fig 7.3 Adjusting the scale gives a graph a different appearance.

Making a visual impact

The first graph in Fig 7.3 appears to indicate that the annual change in the contribution of manufacturing to Singapore's GDP has varied considerably over the period 1975-1984. The second graph, which starts at zero, shows clearly that the change has been slow. In fact the two graphs provide identical information, but because Fig. 7.3 (a) does not start at zero it is possible to give a distorted presentation of the information. On the other hand, starting at zero means that the impact on the reader is lost. The solution is to make a break in the vertical axis just above 0. Doing this will make it clear to the reader that you are not trying to mislead him. See Fig 7.4.

Percentage contribution of manufacturing to Singapore's GDP

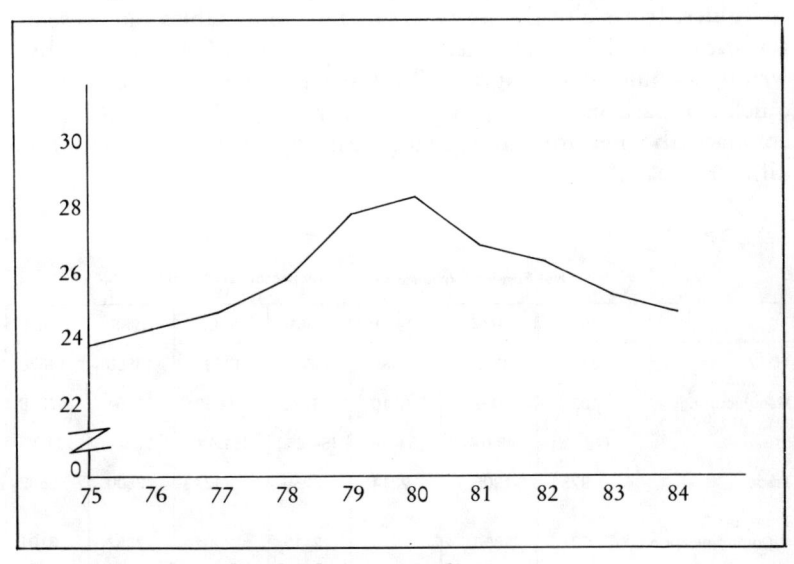

Fig 7.4 Graph with a broken vertical axis.

What types of illustrations are there?

There are:

- Tables
- Graphs
- Pie charts
- Bar charts
- Pictograms
- Drawings
- Photographs
- Maps
- Organisational diagrams

Tables. It has already been shown above how tables can present statistical information in a clearer and more digestible form than by writing a connected paragraph. Tables enable the reader to make a quick comparison of the data given. From Fig. 7.5 it is possible to compare the net foreign exchange earnings per sector and for different years.

Net Foreign Exchange Earnings by Sector ($Million)

	1973	1978	1980	1981	1982	1983	1984
TOTAL	3788	8252	11486	12514	12891	13550	14578
Manufacturing	1835	4007	6210	6785	6630	7164	7978
	(48.4%)	(48.6%)	(54.1%)	(54.2%)	(51.4%)	(52.9%)	(54.7%)
Trade	975	1905	2214	2256	2427	2500	2532
Transport & Communication	737	1856	2376	2719	3004	2987	3101
Financial & Business Services	190	420	583	636	696	749	808
Others	51	64	103	118	134	150	159

Source: "Economic Survey of Singapore, First Quarter 1985" by the Ministry of Trade & Industry.

Fig 7.5 A clearly drawn table.

Making a visual impact

Presentation of the tables must provide clarity and so the number and location of lines is important. Compare Figs 7.6 and 7.7 with Fig 7.5. Which is the clearest?

Net Foreign Exchange Earnings by Sector ($Million)

	1973	1978	1980	1981	1982	1983	1984
TOTAL	3788	8252	11486	12514	12891	13550	14578
Manufacturing	1835	4007	6210	6785	6630	7164	7978
	(48.4%)	(48.6%)	(54.1%)	(54.2%)	(51.4%)	(52.9%)	(54.7%)
Trade	975	1905	2214	2256	2427	2500	2532
Transport & Communication	737	1856	2376	2719	3004	2987	3101
Financial & Business Services	190	420	583	636	696	749	808
Others	51	64	103	118	134	150	159

Source: "Economic Survey of Singapore, First Quarter 1985" by the Ministry of Trade & Industry.

Fig 7.6 A table with each statistic in a box.

Net Foreign Exchange Earnings by Sector ($Million)

	1973	1978	1980	1981	1982	1983	1984
TOTAL	3788	8252	11486	12514	12891	13550	14578
Manufacturing	1835	4007	6210	6785	6630	7164	7978
	(48.4%)	(48.6%)	(54.1%)	(54.2%)	(51.4%)	(52.9%)	(54.7%)
Trade	975	1905	2214	2256	2427	2500	2532
Transport & Communication	737	1856	2376	2719	3004	2987	3101
Financial & Business Services	190	420	583	636	696	749	808
Others	51	64	103	118	134	150	159

Source: "Economic Survey of Singapore, First Quarter 1985" by the Ministry of Trade & Industry.

Fig 7.7 A table with no lines.

The Complete Asian Report Writer

In Fig 7.6 every row is marked off to form a box for each statistic. This results in a mass of criss-cross lines. The effect of the lines is to take your attention away from the figures. In Fig 7.7 there are no lines at all and this makes it difficult to locate the relevant information. The original presentation, Fig 7.5, is the clearest because there are sufficient lines to enable the reader to scan down the columns and the whole table is contained in a box, yet there are not too many lines.

Graphs. Graphs show trends and these trends can make a strong and immediate impact on the reader. He only needs to glance at a graph to see whether there has been a sharp rise or fall in the company's sales performance for example.

When there are two or more lines on a graph it can serve a similar purpose to tables in making a comparison. However, each variable (i.e. each line) must be clearly distinguished from the other one(s) by means of colour or a differently marked line. See Fig 7.8.

Remember, of course, to label each line or to provide a key or legend to indicate what each line represents. And do not forget to

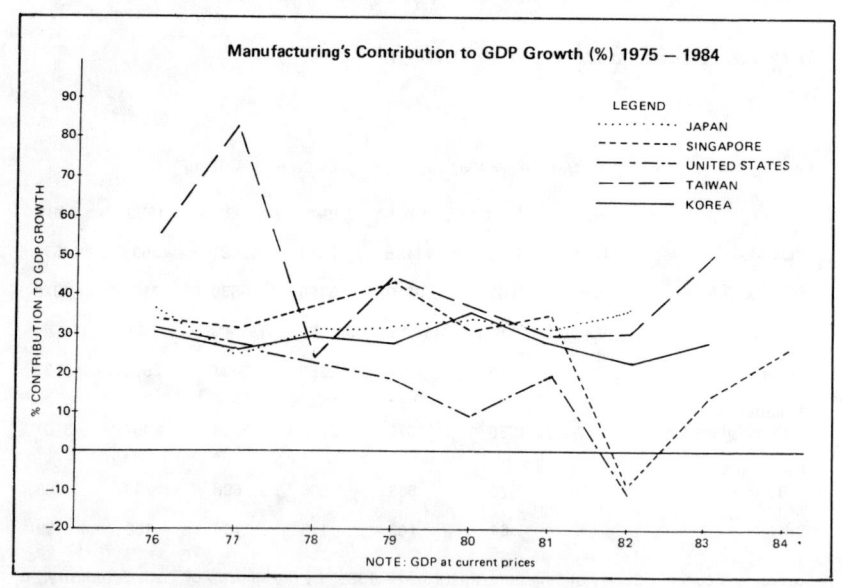

Fig 7.8 A graph with clearly distinguished lines.
(Source: 'What Else Can We Learn from the Japanese?', National Productivity Board, Singapore)

Making a visual impact

label the horizontal (X) and vertical (Y) axes. Everything must be done to ensure that your graphs are clear and unambiguous.

Pie charts. Pie charts have this name because an imaginary pie is divided into pieces. The size of each piece corresponds to its approximate percentage in relation to the whole pie. Thus pie charts serve to indicate the contribution made by different sectors or the various costs in making up the total figure. See Fig 7.9.

Major types of activities supported by the IAEA's technical co-operation programme, 1985 (in thousands of US dollars)

- Industry & Hydrology $4625 — 13.7%
- Agriculture $7104.3 — 21.1%
- Medicine $3178.9 — 9.4%
- Other $2471.6 — 7.3%
- Reactor technology $4710.8 — 14%
- General $3218.7 — 9.5%
- Physics $3809.1 — 11.3%
- Safety $4597.5 — 13.6%

Where were IAEA technical co-operation resources spent in 1985? (in thousands of US dollars)

- Asia & Pacific $9528.3 — 28.4%
- Africa $7005.7 — 20.9%
- Interregional $4482.8 — 13.4%
- Middle East & Europe $4935.2 — 14.7%
- Latin America $7602.5 — 22.7%

(Source: IAEA Bulletin, 1/1987)

Staff Strength

TIBS had altogether 1,117 employees as at 31 December 1986. This comprised 256 administrative and traffic personnel including time-keepers and ticket inspectors out in the field (23 per cent). Others were 155 workshop and store personnel (14 per cent), and 706 bus crew (63 per cent).

- Bus crew 63%
- Administrative and Traffic 23%
- Workshop and Store 14%

(Source: Trans-Island Bus Services Ltd., Singapore. Annual report.)

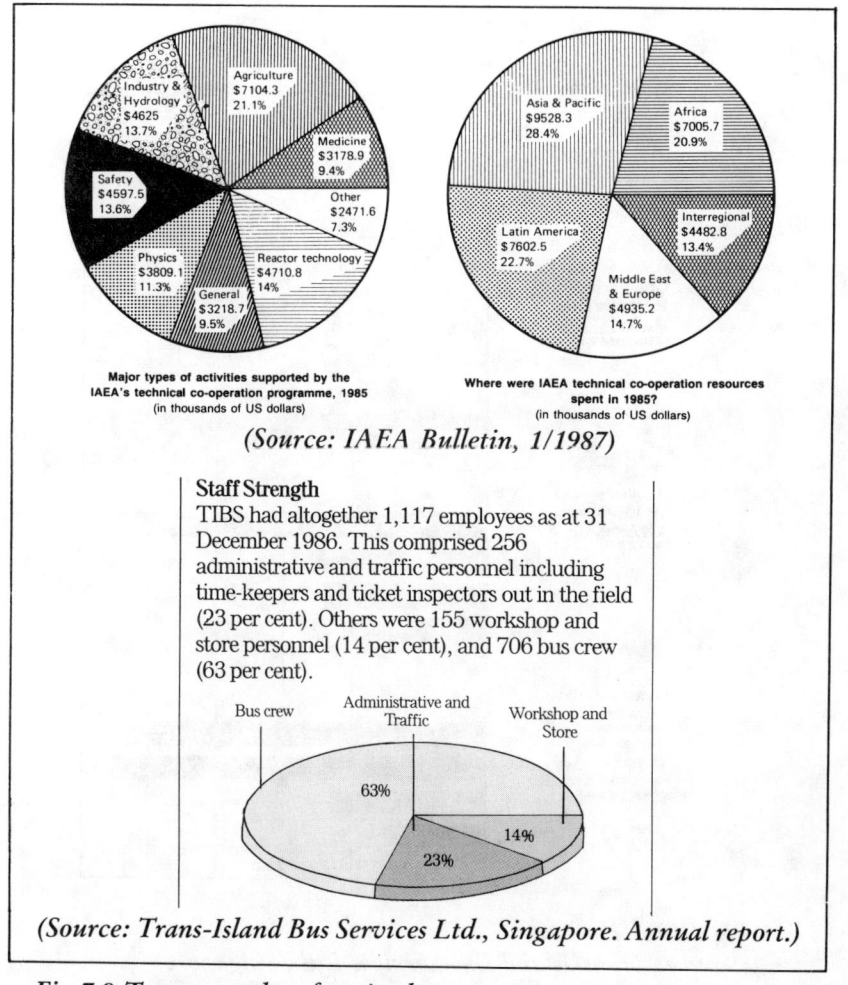

Fig 7.9 Two examples of a pie chart.

The Complete Asian Report Writer

Operational Highlights
营业状况

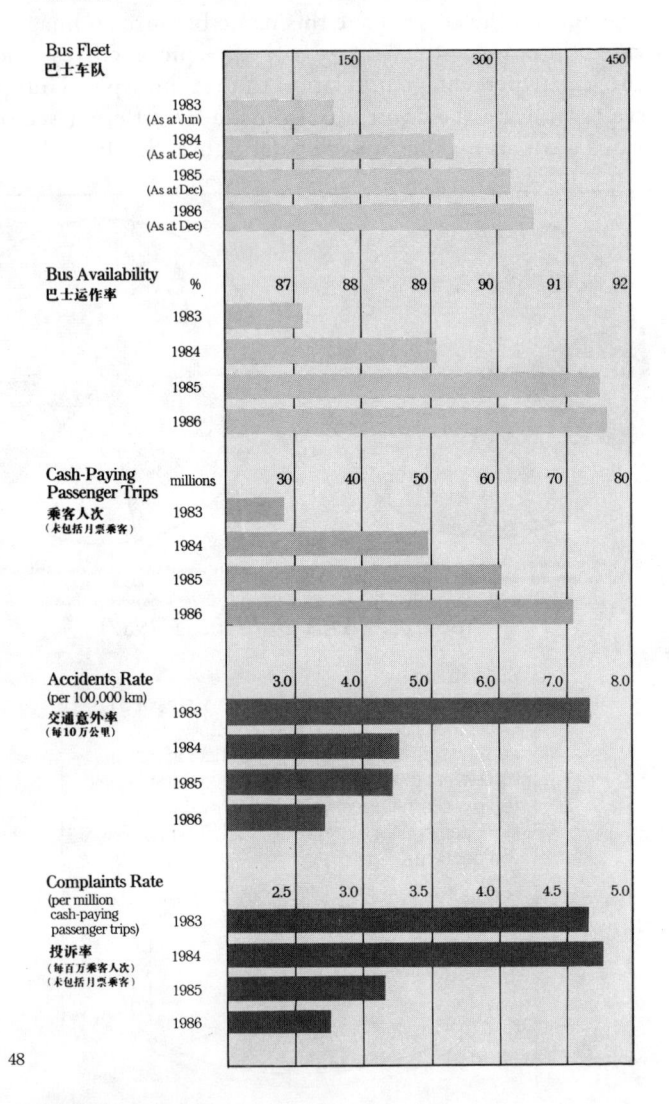

Bus Fleet 巴士车队
- 1983 (As at Jun)
- 1984 (As at Dec)
- 1985 (As at Dec)
- 1986 (As at Dec)

Scale: 150, 300, 450

Bus Availability 巴士运作率 (%)
Scale: 87, 88, 89, 90, 91, 92
- 1983
- 1984
- 1985
- 1986

Cash-Paying Passenger Trips 乘客人次（未包括月票乘客） (millions)
Scale: 30, 40, 50, 60, 70, 80
- 1983
- 1984
- 1985
- 1986

Accidents Rate (per 100,000 km) 交通意外率（每10万公里）
Scale: 3.0, 4.0, 5.0, 6.0, 7.0, 8.0
- 1983
- 1984
- 1985
- 1986

Complaints Rate (per million cash-paying passenger trips) 投诉率（每百万乘客人次）（未包括月票乘客）
Scale: 2.5, 3.0, 3.5, 4.0, 4.5, 5.0
- 1983
- 1984
- 1985
- 1986

48

Fig 7.10 A bar chart.
(Source: Trans-Island Bus Services Ltd., Singapore. Annual report 1986)

Making a visual impact

Certain precautions need to be taken to ensure that the pie chart is presented clearly and accurately.

Firstly, the size of the piece of the pie must be a fairly accurate reflection of its percentage, because pie charts create a general impression on the reader and he will be misled if the size does not correspond to the percentage.

Secondly, the exact percentages should be stated so that the reader can make an exact comparison.

Thirdly, the pie chart is much clearer if each piece of the pie is either coloured or shaded differently, as in Fig 7.9.

Bar charts or histograms. The benefits of bar charts or histograms are that they provide the reader with a general impression together with fairly precise figures, thereby enabling him to make an immediate comparison.

As with the other illustrations each bar and axis must be clearly labelled. See Fig 7.10.

Pictograms. Pictograms are basically bar charts presented in a more dramatic manner to create a lasting impression on the reader. This is achieved by means of pictures which in some way relate to the content of the pictogram.

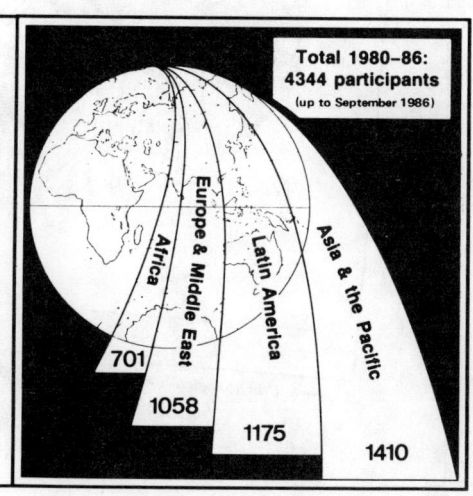

Fig 7.11 A pictogram.
(Source: IAEA Bulletin, 1/1987.)

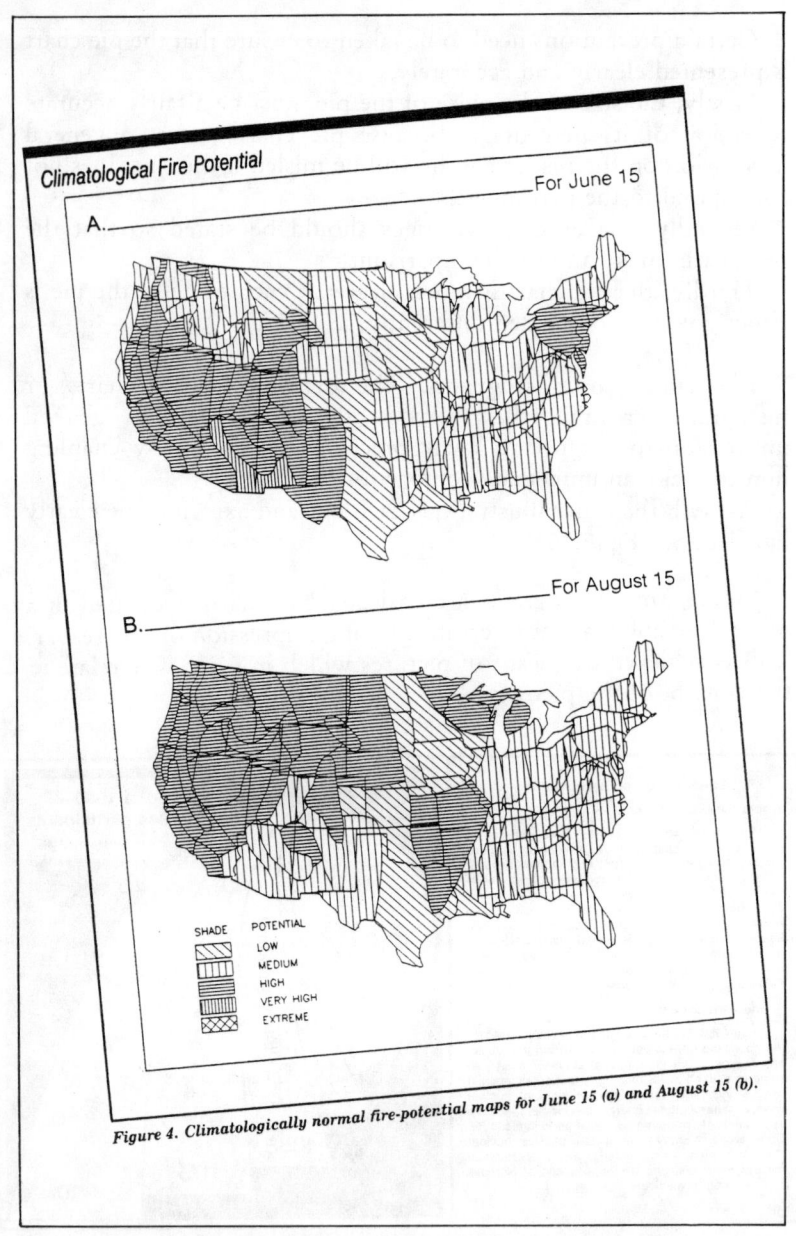

*Fig. 7.12 Map showing fire potential.
(Source: Journal of Forestry, January 1988).*

Making a visual impact

Drawings. When the reader needs to be familiar with the physical structure of a piece of machinery in order to understand how it works, then a drawing is essential. You must also decide what type of drawing is most appropriate to your purpose — an exploded drawing to show small parts on a larger scale, or a cross-sectional drawing to give the reader a new perspective of the interior of the object.

Photographs. Photographs of a piece of equipment for a technical report are not necessarily better than a drawing, however good the photographer. In photographs there may be unnecessary detail which might be confusing, whereas such detail can be omitted from a drawing.

On the other hand, a good photograph can provide invaluable evidence for reports. 'Good' means that it must be **relevant** to the appropriate section of the report and it must be **conclusive** in providing the evidence that you are claiming it gives. In practice, photographs are generally placed in the Appendix and referred to in the body of the report.

Maps. When geographical information is required a map can display it more clearly than words, a table or other types of illustration. Remember, though, that maps must have a scale and a North point. When there is too much detail on the map the result can be confusing and so only relevant information should be included.

Organisational diagrams. The structure of an organisation can be clearly depicted by means of an organisational diagram, which is basically a more complicated version of a tree diagram. Fig 7.13 shows the personnel administration by function at a departmental store in Singapore.

Flow charts. Flow charts are used to depict a system made up of a series of operations occurring in a certain sequence, such as in converting raw material to a finished product. The flow direction is indicated by arrows, as shown in Fig 7.14.

All the types of illustrations that have been discussed enable you to present both statistical and diagrammatic information in your report in a clearer, more dynamic way. However, the illustrations must all have captions and be properly labelled so that the reader can identify what the illustration is describing.

PERSONNEL ADMINISTRATION AT YAOHAN

The Personnel Department is one of the three departments under the Administration Head office. Figure 10 illustrates the organisation of the Personnel Department by functions.

Figure 10 - Functions of Yaohan's Personnel Department

```
                    Personnel Department
                   /                    \
        Personnel Administration    Education and Training
       /         |                    |              
Manpower    Recruitment          Staff Evaluation
Planning        ↓                 ↓            ↓
           Recruitment Exercise  Self Evaluation  Performance Appraisal
                ↓                 ↓                ↓
            Examination         Interview      Promotion Examination
                ↓                 ↓                ↓
            Essay-writing    Transfer, if        Interview
                ↓             necessary            ↓
             Selection                          Promotion
                ↓
             Placement
```

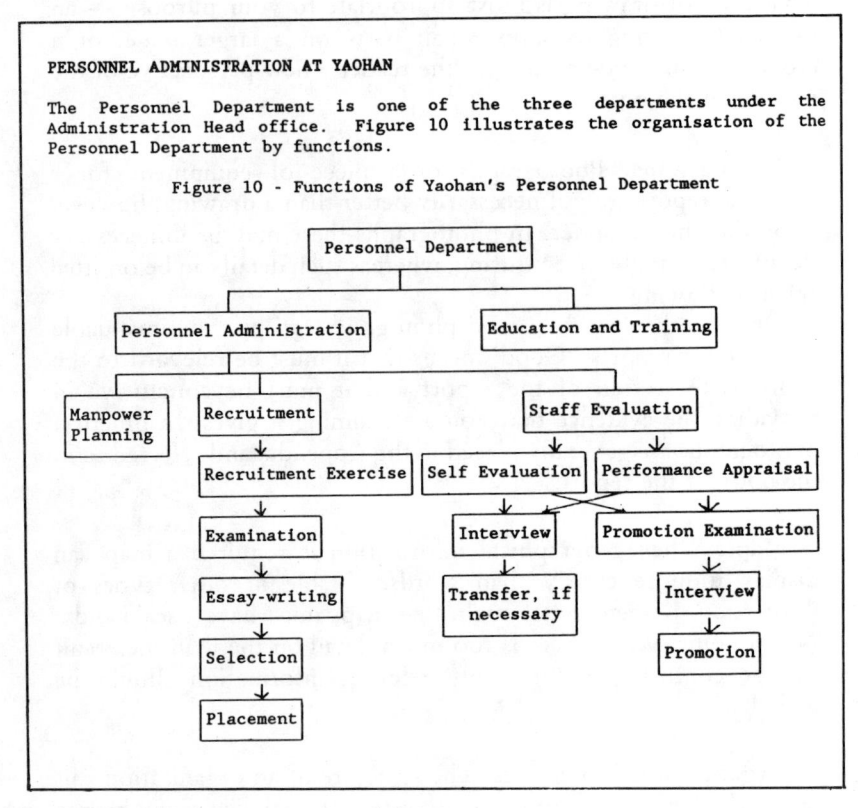

Fig. 7.13 An organisational diagram.
(Source: 'What Else Can We Learn from the Japanese?', National Productivity Board, Singapore.)

Where shall I put my illustration?

You have a choice between the appendix (or annex) and the body of the report. When the illustration is essential to the understanding of the report it should be placed in the body. Otherwise it would be better to place it as an appendix for the reader's reference, for there it will not distract the reader from the report's line of thought.

Making a visual impact

In addition, if the illustration is large, such as a map, it should be placed as an appendix. Nevertheless, all illustrations must be referred to in the text. Further details on appendices are to be found in Chapter 4.

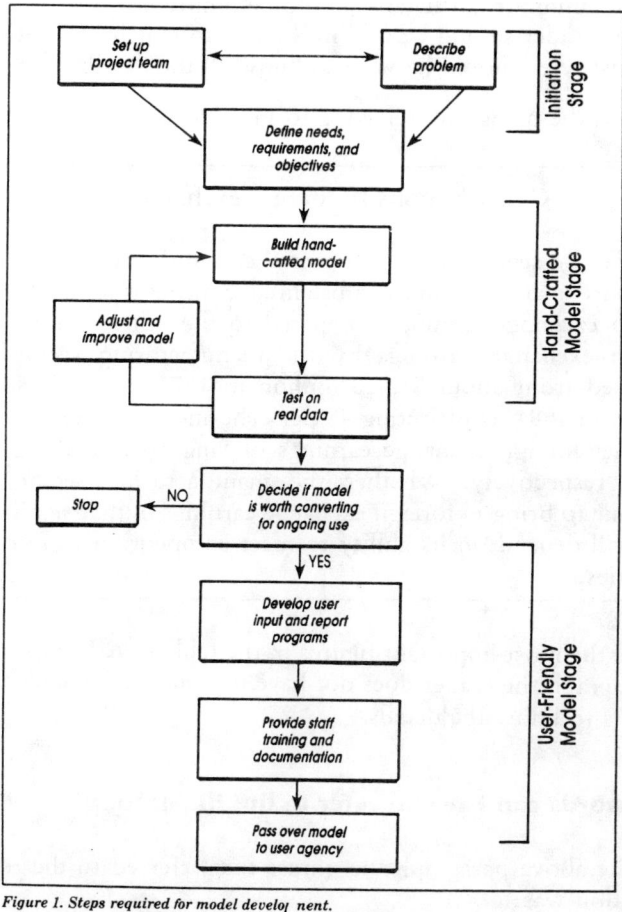

Figure 1. Steps required for model development.

Fig 7.14 A flow chart.
Source: Journal of Forestry, February 1988.)

The Complete Asian Report Writer

How do I write the paragraph that refers to the illustration?

There are three important points to note:

1. The significant points from the illustration should be stated in the text.
2. The unimportant details should be omitted.
3. The reader should be told in the text to which illustration he must refer should he wish to know all the details.

Here is the paragraph referring to Fig 7.5.

Contributions to foreign exchange

'It can be seen from Fig. 2 that the manufacturing sector in Singapore made the most substantial contribution to her net foreign exchange earnings compared to the other sectors. Net foreign exchange earnings by the manufacturing sector had increased from about $1,800 million in 1973 to about $8,000 million in 1984, constituting 48 per cent and 55 per cent of the total net foreign exchange earnings of Singapore in those two years, respectively. Whether the manufacturing sector will continue to bring in foreign exchange earnings in that significant way will depend on its ability to meet competition from other countries.'

Since the most important figures in the table have been stated in the paragraph the reader does not have to examine the table unless he wants to know the details.

What words can I use to refer to the illustration?

In the above paragraph the phrase that referred to the relevant illustration was:

'It can be seen from Fig 2 that ...'

Other suitable phrases are:

Making a visual impact

According to ⎫
As shown in ⎬ Fig 3, inflation ⎧ reached a peak ⎫
As can be seen from ⎭   ⎨ peaked ⎬ in 1988.
                         ⎩ rose sharply ⎭

Fig. 3 ⎧ indicates that ⎫ inflation rose sharply in 1988.
       ⎨ shows that   ⎬
       ⎩   ⎭

Fig 2 ⎧ indicates ⎫ a ⎛ gradual ⎞ ⎛ increase ⎞ in sales.
      ⎨ shows   ⎬   ⎜ steady ⎟ ⎜ rise   ⎟
      ⎩   ⎭   ⎜ rapid   ⎟ ⎜ fall   ⎟
                      ⎜ sudden ⎟ ⎜ decline ⎟
                      ⎜ sharp   ⎟ ⎝ drop   ⎠
                      ⎝ steep   ⎠

The steady increase in sales ⎧ is shown   ⎫ in ⎧ Fig 2. ⎫
                             ⎨ is illustrated⎬   ⎨ the graph below. ⎬

SUMMARY

In presenting your report as clearly as possible to the reader and at the same time making a strong visual impact on him, you must pay attention to **layout** and **illustrations**. It may take time to make sure that you have chosen the most suitable method of presenting statistical or diagrammatic information, but it is vital that you make use of the various means at your disposal to communicate the information to the reader.

Remember though that each illustration must have a caption, and axes, rows etc. must be labelled. This will help to ensure clarity, which is an essential quality of reports.

8 Writing the conclusion

WHAT IS A CONCLUSION?

> **con·clusion** /kən'kluːʒn/ *n* [C] **1** end: *at the ~ of his speech; bring a matter to a speedy ~.* **in ~,** lastly. **2** arranging; deciding; settling (*of*): *the ~ of a peace treaty.* **3** belief or opinion which is the result of reasoning: *come to/reach the ~ that ... ; to draw a ~ (from evidence, etc).* **a foregone ~,** something settled or decided in advance, not to be doubted.

(Oxford Advanced Learner's Dictionary of English)

Two meanings are applicable to report writing:

1. End
2. Belief or opinion which is the result of reasoning.

End

The conclusion of a report is written after you have finished the body of the report. Since the body contains all the details, the conclusion should contain **no** new information. It may, however, **briefly summarise** the main points so that the reader is reminded of the essential information and then he can evaluate the logical

Writing the conclusion

deductions you make. This summary must be brief because the reader does not want to re-read your report in the conclusion.

Belief based on reasoning

After writing the body of the report, and perhaps a summary of the main points, you should be able to make **logical deductions** based on the information you have presented.

It is important that they are logical, meaning that they must be 'correctly reasoned'. Your report may be well researched and planned, and written extremely clearly, but if you then make an illogical deduction, you will have ruined all the good work.

The deductions are important because the recommendations follow on automatically from them, and management makes decisions based on them. Illogical deductions will therefore be detrimental to your company and to your own future. For this reason, never jump to a conclusion — it may be a wrong one because you lack an essential piece of information. Always make sure you have all the relevant facts so that you can make an informed and logical deduction.

The body of the report must be objective, and your conclusions, though to some extent subjective, must be based on the evidence you have presented and not on your wishes or prior prejudices.

IS THIS LOGICAL?

The following letter was taken from the Forum page of Singapore's English-language newspaper, The Straits Times. The writer is commenting on a Reuter report on the collapse of the Hotel New World building.

> 'I fully support the Government's decision to expel the Reuter correspondent responsible for a damaging report about rescue efforts at the Hotel New World disaster site.
>
> I was in Bangkok when I read the report and was tempted to check with our embassy there as to its accuracy. I am glad the Government had the courage to react speedily to the report.
>
> It is hoped that more can be done to erase the poor publicity we received overseas, especially to counter the snide and

spurious articles that were printed on the disaster.
So much for the honest investigative and probing nature of the media!
The media in Singapore may not be one which is very investigative — simply because there isn't much to investigate — but I do hope that it maintains its honest, balanced and unsensational reporting.'

Subjectivity is generally present when adjectives that make value judgments are used. Note the adjectives used:

'snide', 'spurious' for non-Singaporean articles;
'honest, balanced and unsensational' for Singaporean articles.

Is there proof to support these adjectives? In other words, is the writer's opinion based on sound reasoning?

It appears from the letter that the writer based his comments on that one article written by the Reuter correspondent. How could he make a general comment on articles published overseas? Was he in Singapore and at the site of the disaster? Did he know all the facts? Since he could not answer 'yes' to these questions, he was not in a position to describe Singapore reports of the disaster as 'honest, balanced, and unsensational'.

Deductions must be based on reason, and this means the facts must be presented first. Subjective adjectives tend to indicate too great an emphasis on personal opinion, and thus your conclusion will sound less rather than more convincing.

WHERE SHALL I PUT THE CONCLUSION?

There are four methods of structuring the report:

1.
```
INTRODUCTION
BODY
CONCLUSION
RECOMMENDATIONS
```

This is the order in which you probably wrote the report. In addition, the reader will probably understand the conclusion better if he has read the introduction and body first, and so this can be regarded as the most logical structure.

2.
> CONCLUSION
> RECOMMENDATIONS
> INTRODUCTION
> BODY

The value of this structure stems from the fact that the reader is mainly interested in your conclusions and recommendations, since these sections will provide the basis for his possible actions. After he has read these two sections, he can decide whether to read on and find out all the details on which the conclusion is based.

By placing the conclusion and recommendations at the beginning of the report, the reader can locate them immediately, and will not have to spend time looking for them.

3.
> INTRODUCTION
> CONCLUSION
> RECOMMENDATION
> BODY

The advantage of this structure is that the reader is given the purpose, scope and background information first. This will enable him to understand the conclusion and recommendations more clearly.

The disadvantage of placing the conclusion before the body is that all the important findings must be included in the conclusion, otherwise the reader will not be able to evaluate your deductions. This can lead to an overly lengthy conclusion. Moreover, the body, which probably took you the longest time to write, may well be ignored.

4.
> SYNOPSIS (Summary)
> INTRODUCTION
> BODY
> CONCLUSION
> RECOMMENDATIONS

This is a compromise of the previous structures. The synopsis or summary (see Chapter 11) will summarise the introduction, the most significant findings, the conclusion and the main recommendations. It should be placed at the beginning of the report and it will serve to save the time of a busy reader.

However, the reader who wants to know all the details and understand how you reached your conclusions, can read the report following the most logical structure i.e. Method 1.

It should be evident that this structure with a synopsis offers the reader flexibility. Certain companies have their own in-house rules for report formats, but if the choice is yours, this is the structure you should choose.

HOW DO I WRITE THE CONCLUSION?

As indicated above, the two primary functions of the conclusion are:

i) to summarise the main findings
ii) to make logical deductions

Good use of connectives (see Chapter 6) is necessary in order to write a clear summary and logical deductions. The information stated in a summary is in condensed form, and so connectives enable the reader to identify each fact. Sequence words (first, second, next, finally), words introducing additional information (not only ... but also, in addition, and), examples (e.g. such as) and contrast (however, on the other hand, whereas) are particularly common.

In addition, connectives indicate the reasoning behind your deductions. Thus, frequently used connectives are those which introduce reasons (because, since) and results (therefore, thus, hence).

Examples
A market research report. (See Chapter 5)

> The results of this survey show that in terms of communication, 'Soccer Special' produced some very encouraging scores. Virtually all respondents were aware that the main message of this commercial was that Shok gives you energy, whereas they gave several different answers concerning the main message of 'Long Distance Sportsman'. On the other hand, 'Long Distance Sportsman' made a greater impact on the respondents, thanks to its song/jingle. Furthermore, its appeal was wider than that of 'Soccer Special' because it was presented as a drink that would nourish the whole family.
>
> It can be concluded therefore, that the 'Long Distance Sportsman' appears to be the more persuasive of the two commercials and is the one that is more 'likely' to lead to increased sales.

2. **An information report**

Conclusion

> Most of Yaohan's practices can be adopted by local business organisations to strive towards greater success. An example is Yaohan's true philosophy of life, which guides the actions of the workers and management in their daily business. This must be supported by the strong structures of good labour-management relations and useful staff contributions, such as in QCC/TQC programmes and staff suggestion meetings. Human resources, being a company's most valuable asset to realise productivity, should be properly trained and moulded to ensure that the best performance is produced. At the same time, there should be equitable rewards for employees to reinforce their desire to perform satisfactorily.
>
> Yaohan's policy of constantly looking from the customers' point of view has also proved effective in coping with environmental changes successfuly. Its efforts in research and implementation of the resultant action plans have also proved fruitful.
>
> (Source: Case study of Yaohan, from 'What Else Can We Learn from the Japanese?')

3. **A recommendation report**

Chapter 4 has an outline of a report entitled 'Photography for Drawings'. Here is the conclusion to that report:

Conclusion

The present method of employing a photographer is proving to be excessively expensive, costing a total of $6,950 per annum for photographs which are of unnecessarily high quality. In addition, there is a delay of a week before we actually receive them.

The proposed method, on the other hand, is convenient, saves personnel time, yet still provides photographs of suitable quality. Moreover, although this system requires an initial outlay of $2,000 to purchase the camera, it would very quickly pay for itself, since over 10 years the annual costs would amount to only $1,975 per annum.

COMMENTS ON THE CONCLUSIONS

1. **A market research report**

The conclusion summarises the results of the survey, thereby enabling the reader to make an easy comparison between the two commercials. This comparison involves the use of connectives that introduce a contrast, e.g. 'whereas', 'on the other hand', and adjectives that could be regarded as subjective e.g. 'very encouraging', 'greater', 'wider', 'more persuasive'. These adjectives, however, are based on the writer's analysis of the results of the survey and so are acceptable.

The concluding sentence is the logical deduction, based on the preceding summary, and this is emphasised by the word 'therefore'.

2. **An information report**

Often there is no attempt to analyse information in this type of report. Thus, there is no deduction, as in the example,

Writing the conclusion

where the conclusion is merely a summary of the main findings.

Note the connectives that are used to introduce:

i) Examples
an example is . . . , such as

ii) Additional information
and, also, at the same time.

3. **A recommendation report**

This conclusion provides a fairly comprehensive summary, using connectives such as 'moreover', 'in addition', to add information. The contrast between the two methods is stressed by 'on the other hand'.

The use of certain subjective adjectives and adverbs, namely 'excessively high', and 'unnecessarily' can be justified provided they are based on sound reasoning. At the end of the summary, there follows a logical deduction, which states that this method 'would very quickly pay for itself'. The reason for this deduction is then introduced by the connective 'since'. It is now very clear what recommendation is going to be made.

The conclusion, therefore, serves to summarise the main findings, make logical deductions and lead the reader to any recommendations that you are going to make.

9 Writing the recommendations

WHAT IS A RECOMMENDATION?

rec·om·mend /ˌrekəˈmend/ vt **1** [VP6A,14,12A, 13A,16A] ~ sth (to sb) (for sth); ~ sb sth; ~ sb (for sth/as sth), speak favourably of; say that one thinks sth is good (for a purpose) or that sb is fitted (for a post, etc, as ...): *I can ~ this soap. He has been ~ed for first class honours. What would you ~ for getting ink stains from my blouse? Can you ~ me a good novel? Can you ~ Miss Hill as a good typist?* **2** [VP17,6C,9] suggest as wise or suitable; advise: *I have been ~ed to try these pills for sea-sickness. I ~ you not to/that you do not disobey your officers. Do you ~ raising the school-leaving age?* **3** [VP6A,14] ~ sb (to sb), (of a quality, etc) cause to be or appear pleasing, satisfactory; make acceptable: *Behaviour of that sort will not ~ you.* **4** [VP14] ~ sb to sb, commend (the more usu word): ~ *oneself/one's soul to God;* ~ *a child to sb's care.* **rec·om·men·da·tion** /ˌrekəmenˈdeɪʃn/ n **1** [U] ~ing: *speak in ~ation of sb or sth; buy sth on the ~ation of a friend, because he has ~ed it.* **2** [C] statement that ~s sb or sth: *My bank manager has sent me a list of ~ations, eg names of stocks which he ~s me to buy. The jury brought in a verdict of guilty, with a ~ation to mercy.* **3** [C] sth which causes a person to be well thought of: *Is a sweet disposition a ~ation in a wife?*

(Oxford Advanced Learner's Dictionary of English.)

Writing the recommendations

It is the second meaning that is applicable to report writing. In other words, 'recommend' means 'suggest as wise or suitable; advise'.

Therefore, a recommendation is 'a statement that suggests something as wise or suitable'.

WHAT IS A SUITABLE RECOMMENDATION?

If the advice that you give is going to be suitable, it must be based on the conclusion that precedes the recommendations. No recommendation should come as a surprise to the reader, because if it does it will not seem logical and so is likely to be rejected immediately. In other words, suitable means 'following logically from the conclusion which in turn has followed **logically** from the body of the report'.

A second aspect of suitability is **relevance**. The recommendations must be within the scope of the report. To ensure that they are relevant, you must refer to the introduction and the terms of reference.

Referring to the introduction and the terms of reference, especially the purpose, will enable you to check your recommendations against the purpose. In this way, you can ensure that they, and therefore your report as a whole, meet the aims of your report. If your recommendations are not sufficiently **comprehensive**, you may have to do more research and analysis.

A suitable recommendation section will therefore be **logical**, **relevant** and **comprehensive**. This will increase the persuasive element of your report and create the right impression on the reader.

DO ALL REPORTS REQUIRE RECOMMENDATIONS?

Those reports which are purely providing information do not require any recommendations. This explains why the 10 case studies in 'What Else Can We Learn from the Japanese?' do not contain a recommendation section.

It should be apparent that the conclusion and recommendation sections are very closely linked. Consequently, in some reports,

131

they are combined under one heading, 'Conclusion and Recommendations'.

There are, however, two distinct differences between the two. Firstly, the conclusion summarises and analyses the facts whereas the recommendations suggest the resulting action that should be taken.

Secondly, the conclusion tends to consider what has already happened or the present situation, whereas the recommendations refer to the future.

These differences partially justify separate sections for the conclusion and recommendations, but the main reason is that a list of recommendations as a separate section makes it easy for the reader to see what action you are suggesting. If he wishes to know all the reasons for the action, he can turn back to the conclusion and the body.

HOW SHOULD I WRITE THE RECOMMENDATIONS?

Briefly. Each recommendation should be written concisely without a mass of supporting information. A reason for the recommendation can be briefly given, but even this may not be necessary since the reason should be apparent in the conclusion.

Clearly. There should be no possible ambiguity that could lead to the implementation of a suggestion that was never made.

Precisely. Vague recommendations frequently result from insufficient research and/or inadequate analysis. An example of an imprecise recommendation is:

'Some machines should be serviced more frequently.'

The reader will immediately think: 'What machinery in particular? How frequently?'

How you write recommendations will be affected by your relationship with the reader and by your knowledge of his opinions on the subject of your report. You may, for example, add an extra sentence to convince the reader that your recommendation is suitable, especially when it contradicts his original ideas on the

Writing the recommendations

subject. You may feel it is not your responsibility to dictate to your boss precise courses of action to be taken, and so you prefer to be a little vague; or perhaps the precise measures to be taken are outside the scope of your report.

However, in spite of these qualifying comments, you should generally strive to write **brief, clear** and **precise** recommendations.

WHAT LANGUAGE SHOULD I USE?

Remembering that you are writing recommendations or suggestions, which of the alternatives do you prefer in the following recommendation that appears at the end of a report on 'Company Absenteeism and Lack of Punctuality'?

> A company bus service must/should/could/may be provided to transport employees from the three main residential areas of Woodlands, Clementi and Toa Payoh to the factory.

'Must' is too strong, sounding like a command rather than a recommendation. On the other hand, 'could' and 'may' are too weak, betraying a lack of certainty on the part of the writer. The best alternative is clearly 'should'.

Notice also how precisely the recommendation has been written, stating the places from which transport should be provided.

Another aspect of language is the choice between the personal 'I/We recommend that ...' and 'It is recommended that ...'

In a very formal report the tendency is to use the impersonal 'It is recommended that ...'. However, if it is a memo report, the personal 'I recommend' is often regarded as preferable. The choice is greatly dependent on in-house customs.

ISN'T PUNCTUATION A PROBLEM SOMETIMES?

If there is only one recommendation, then punctuation is no problem. e.g.

> It is recommended that Sunset Hills be selected as the new site for the school since the land there is considerably cheaper'.

133

Notice that the word 'should' can be omitted after 'It is recommended that ...'. See Appendix 3 for an explanation of the subjunctive.

However, punctuation is not so straightforward when there is more than one recommendation.

Below is the recommendation section from a report entitled 'The Canteen Facilities'. It has been punctuated in two different ways.

1. **Using the colon/semi-colon**

   In view of the current situation regarding the canteen facilities, it is recommended that:

   (a) the variety of food be increased by ensuring that there is Chinese, Muslim, Indian and Western food available each day;

   (b) hygiene be improved by employing one additional canteen worker to clear and clean the tables; and

   (c) delays at the cash register be reduced by introducing a second cash register.

   Notice that the introduction to the list of recommendations ends with a colon. This means that the first recommendation that follows starts with a lower case letter. Each recommendation, except the last one, ends with a semi-colon and so the next one also starts with a lower case letter.

2. **Using full-stops**

   In view of the current situation regarding the canteen facilities, the following measures are recommended.

   (a) The variety of food should be increased by ensuring that there is Chinese, Muslim, Indian and Western food available each day.

   (b) Hygiene should be improved by employing one additional canteen worker to clear and clean the tables.

Writing the recommendations

(c) Delays at the cash register should be reduced by introducing a second cash register.

Note that with the full-stops, each recommendation is a complete sentence. Therefore each one starts with a capital letter and requires 'should' in the sentence.

Examples

1. **A market research report.** (See Chapters 5 and 8)

---

4. Recommendations

We wish to make the following recommendations regarding the two commercials, 'Soccer Special' and 'Long Distance Sportsman'.

   4.1 The older 'Soccer Special' commercial should be dropped, even from soccer playing countries, since it has failed to make a sufficiently strong impact on the whole community.
   4.2 In the next advertising campaign, the new 'Long Distance Sportsman' should be used throughout the Asean region, in view of its persuasiveness and wide appeal.
   4.3 The results of the next advertising campaign should be analysed carefully to determine the success of the campaign and whether one particular aspect of Shok needs to be highlighted.

---

2. **Report of a consultative committee.**

The report of Singapore's Property Market Consultative Committee is entitled 'Action Plan for the Property Sector'. The title alone indicates that there will be many recommendations. One particular aspect of this report concerns property developers in relation to market organisation. Here are the recommendations.

> In consultation with the Urban Redevelopment Authority (URA), we recommend the following measures:
>
> (a) an additional five-year moratorium on land premium repayments commencing from 1 January 1986;
>
> (b) an extension of completion time of up to five years after the 35 per cent extension time (discussed earlier);
>
> (c) an adjustment in interest rate, on outstanding land premia, to the average prime rate of the four big local banks, with effect from 1 January 1986;
>
> (d) the payment, on request by individual developers, of half of the interest during the moratorium and capitalisation of the remaining half; and
>
> (e) the imposition of liquidated damages, if any, at the end of the project instead of at different stages of completion.

3. **A recommendation report.** (See Chapters 8 and 12.)

The writer is obliged to recommend a cheaper method of obtaining photographs for drawings.

> 5. Recommendation
>
> It is recommended that an instant camera be purchased to enable us to take our own photographs, thereby saving the company $4,975 per annum over 10 years.

4. **A feasibility report**

Below is the recommendation section to a feasibility study on the setting up of a business school. In the conclusion, the writers have indicated that a need exists for such a school and that the project is operationally viable.

8. Recommendations

In order to provide a sound foundation for the school, we make the following recommendations.

8.1 Specialised consultants should be employed to search for and recommend a suitable candidate for the position of school principal.

8.2 The teachers should be placed on a higher salary scale than is currently found in the country. This will attract and hold a well-motivated and effective teaching staff.

8.3 Student fees should be set at US$1,500 per annum, which is the mid-range compared with typical institutions which might be similar to the school.

8.4 An examination system should be used, leading to full or partial diplomas or other qualifications. (See Section 6.2 for further details)

COMMENTS

1. **A market research report.**

Note the numbering system that has been used. Since in this report the recommendation section is 4, then each recommendation can be numbered 4.1, 4.2, etc. This makes it very easy for the reader to note the number of recommendations you have made. Since each recommendation is a complete sentence, capital letters, full-stops and 'should' are required.

The recommendations follow logically from the conclusion, where it was stated that 'Long Distance Sportsman' was more persuasive and had wider appeal. The objectives of the report, which required a recommendation concerning which commercial to use in future advertising campaigns, are also fulfilled.

It is also apparent that the order in which the recommendations were written is logical. The recommendation to use 'Long Distance Sportsman' must come after the one to drop 'Soccer Special'.

2. Report of a consultative committee.

Each recommendation is brief, yet precise. The first one, for example, states the length of the additional moratorium on land repayments and the date from which it should take effect.

The punctuation is a colon and semi-colons, with lower case letters. Each recommendation is an incomplete sentence starting with a noun phrase following on from 'we recommend'.

> We recommend . . . an additional five-year moratorium
> . . . an extension of completion time of up to five years
> . . . an adjustment in interest rate

When recommendations are listed in this way, it is imperative that each recommendation fit (note the use of the subjunctive!) grammatically with the introductory 'We recommend' or 'It is recommended that . . . ' In addition, the grammatical structure of each recommendation should be similar. For example, in the above, each one starts with a noun phrase. It could have been a clause

> We recommend that ... the moratorium on land repayments be continued for an additional five years
> ... the completion time be extended by up to five years
> ... the interest rate be adjusted

Whether you choose a noun phrase or a clause, you must be consistent by using the same structure for each recommendation in your list, thereby observing parallel structure.

3. **A recommendation report.**

It is clear from the conclusion which method is going to be recommended. Therefore the recommendation merely states the obvious and then briefly justifies that choice.

4. **A feasibility report.**

The main recommendation — whether or not the project is feasible and economically viable — is in the conclusion section. As a consequence, the recommendation section, which deals with implementation of the project, refers back to the main body of the report rather than to the conclusion.

If there are no recommendations concerning implementation, the feasibility or non-feasibility of the project would be the sole recommendation in this section.

Note that each recommendation is a complete sentence, stating exactly what is being recommended followed by a brief justification.

Remember to make your recommendations logical, relevant and comprehensive. Then write them briefly, clearly, and precisely, paying careful attention to punctuation and language.

10 Revising your report

You have written the first draft of your report and it is tempting to stop there with a sigh of relief that the report is finished. If you have followed all the advice given in the research, planning, writing and presentation stages of preparing a report, then your report will be a good one. Unfortunately though, first efforts are never perfect and there will always be room for improvement. Revision is essential. There are three methods of revising your report.

READ IT AGAIN

If you have organised your time schedule appropriately, you should have completed your first draft a few days before the report has to be submitted. This will enable you to put the report aside for 24 or 48 hours before re-reading it. The advantage of waiting is that the delay enables you to be more objective. Assuming you are pleased with what you have written, you are unlikely to see many areas requiring improvement if you re-read the report immediately. The delay will allow you to come with a clear, fresh mind to the report and so you may well see where improvements are needed and how to make them.

In order to re-read your report objectively, you must put yourself in the position of the reader. This means reading it as if you had the same background and technical knowledge as this reader. As you read, ask yourself the question 'Is the report absolutely clear?' If you have made certain assumptions about the reader's knowledge, these should become evident and you will know what changes to make.

Revising your report

Another aspect of reading objectively is to forget your own attitudes to the subject and the conclusions you have drawn. As you read the report, check that the body contains facts rather than opinions, and that the conclusion is logically drawn from the information that is presented. In addition, if you believe that the reader may not agree with your conclusion you will have to be particularly convincing. As you re-read the conclusion, you should ask yourself, 'Have I been convinced that this conclusion is acceptable?'

When we write, we sometimes have thoughts that we do not find easy to express clearly in words. Rather than lose the thought we express it the best we can. We know what we mean and so the thought is clear to us, but will it be clear to the reader? Re-reading your report a few days later enables you to check the clarity of expression. Furthermore, you may see certain repetitions and realise how you could write a sentence more concisely.

Naturally, such revision is easily carried out when the report is written on a word-processor. You can move paragraphs around and edit sentences with the minimum of inconvenience. This little bit of additional work is worthwhile if it results in the report having a greater impact on the reader.

USE A CHECKLIST

The questions that have just been mentioned are those which must be asked to ensure the reader's full and quick understanding of your report. There are many other questions that you must consider in order to check that the report is well written and achieves its objectives. These questions form the checklist below.

1. **Purpose**

   Will the reader understand the purpose clearly?

   What to do: Check the title, synopsis and introduction.

2. **Reader**

   a) Does the reader have sufficient background information for him to understand the report?

b) Have I considered the reader in the amount of technical terminology I have used?

What to do: Put yourself in the position of the reader, with his background and technical knowledge, and make sure the report is clear and easy to understand.

3. **Information**

   a) Is my report complete? Have I included all the necessary information?

   What to do: Check through your notes to make sure nothing relevant has been omitted. Also go through your different sources and see if there are others that you have forgotten.

   b) Have I included only relevant information?

   What to do: Remove anything you decide is not relevant to the purpose of the report or to the intended reader.

   c) Have I included only accurate information?

   What to do: Check that your sources are reliable and objective and that the information is up-to-date.

4. **Organisation**

   Have I organised the topics in the best way?

   What to do: Check that all the sub-headings are related to the main heading. Make sure that no sub-heading would fit in better elsewhere.

5. **Ordering**

   a) Is my reasoning logical to the reader?
   b) Is there a logical progression in the presentation of information?

   What to do: Check that your thinking is logical within each section and within the report as a whole. First of all, make sure that the examples and details you provide support the point you are making. If the reasoning is not logical you will have to find additional information so that there is no missing step in the logical line of thought. If such information cannot be found, a major revision will be necessary.

If the report as a whole is not written in a logical order you must consider changing the order in which information is presented so that the report is clear and easy for the reader to understand.

6. **Layout**

Does the layout make the information clear and easy for the reader to understand?

What to do: Check that the paragraphing, spacing, headings and numbering system enhance the report's readability. A second check will be needed after typing to ensure that the margins and spacing make the layout attractive to the eye.

7. **Illustrations**

   a) Is there any information that could be more clearly presented by means of an illustration rather than words?
   b) Have I chosen the most suitable type of illustration to present the information?
   c) Is each illustration relevant?
   d) Have I labelled and captioned the illustrations?
   e) Have I referred to the illustrations in the text?

What to do: Remember that illustrations present statistics clearer than words do, but make sure that each illustration achieves its intended purpose. For example, if the purpose is to show a trend, then a graph is more suitable than a table. Check also that each illustration is relevant to the purpose of the report, the axes and columns etc. are labelled and that the illustration has a caption. Then read the text to check that you have referred to the illustration and picked out the significant points.

8. Diction

a) Have I used words which convey my intended meaning?
b) Am I sure that the connotations of the words are the ones I want to express?
c) Have I any doubts about the spelling of any words?
d) Will the reader understand the words I have used?

What to do: Use a dictionary to check the meanings and spellings of words. Be sure that your words are familiar to the reader.

9. Grammar, punctuation

a) Is the grammar correct?
b) Are there any ambiguities?
c) Does my punctuation make the meaning clear?

What to do: Check that there are no grammatical mistakes and watch for ambiguities. Waiting a few days before checking will enable you to notice errors more easily. If you are concerned about your grammar, you can ask a colleague to check your report. (See section Ask a Colleague, on Page 148.)

10. Conciseness

Have I been long-winded?

What to do: Check that you have not unnecessarily repeated words, added superfluous words and sentences or used circumlocutions.

11. Clarity

Is the report clear to the reader?

What to do: Since clarity is so important you must put yourself in the position of the intended reader and decide whether the information, organisation and language will be clear to him. From the language point of view check that your

Revising your report

sentences are not too long, your words are familiar, parallel constructions have been used where appropriate, no ambiguities are present, and that your writing is cohesive.

12. **Conclusion**

    a) Have I accidentally included any new information in the conclusion?

    What to do: Assuming that this information is important you must include it in the body of the report in the appropriate section. If it will not fit into any section you will have to add a new one. Remember that no new information should be put in the conclusion.

    b) Have I summarised only the main points?

    What to do: The conclusion should not be too long and so you must remove any points that you decide are not important.

    c) Are my deductions logical?

    What to do: Read each deduction carefully and then go back to the body of the report to check that there is sufficient information for you to make such a deduction.

13. **Recommendations**

    a) Are my recommendations logical?

    What to do: Check that each recommendation follows logically from the conclusion.

    b) Is each recommendation clear?

    What to do: Check that the recommendation is stated precisely so that the reader knows exactly what you recommend.

    c) Do the recommendations achieve the purpose of the report?

What to do: Refer to the terms of reference and to your statement of the report's purpose in the introduction. Ask yourself whether your recommendations will solve the problem, or guide the reader in making a certain decision etc.

14. **Appendices**

    a) Should I move any illustration from the body of the report to the appendix or vice versa?

    What to do: Decide whether the information contained in the illustration is too long and detailed for the body, or contains a large amount of indirectly relevant information which would not interest every reader. If so, use an appendix.

    b) Are all the appendices necessary?

    c) Have I referred to them in the text?

    What to do: Make sure all the appendices bear some relevance to the report. This can be checked by looking at the body of the report to make sure you referred to them in the text. If you made no reference to an appendix it is a sign that the information it contains is not necessary.

15. **Sources**

    Have I acknowledged my sources of information?

    What to do: Check that you have stated the sources of any information that you have included in your report.

16. **Title page**

    a) Is the title precise and accurate?
    b) Is the title page attractively set out?
    c) Does it contain all the necessary information?

    What to do: Make sure the title page creates a positive impression on the reader by checking that the answer to each of the above questions is 'yes'.

Revising your report

17. **Table of contents**

    a) Have I included one?
    b) Does it match the headings and sub-headings included in my report?

    What to do: For a long report a table of contents is necessary, and so you must go through your report to make sure it matches exactly the headings and sub-headings.

18. **Bibliography**

    a) Do I need one?
    b) Have I stated the necessary details?

    What to do: If you have made use of any books or journals you should include a bibliography. Check that you have stated the title, author, publishers and date of publication so that the reader of your report can make reference to the relevant book if he wishes to do so.

19. **Synopsis**

    a) Have I stated the purpose?
    b) Does the synopsis enable the reader to understand the essential aspects of the report?
    c) Is the synopsis well structured?

    What to do: Make sure that no important fact has been omitted, and that the synopsis accurately summarises the purpose, the main findings, the conclusion and the recommendations. In addition, ensure that there is a logical link between the selected findings and your conclusions, and that the recommendations achieve the stated purpose. In other words, the synopsis should be able to stand alone as a brief yet coherent report.

Nos. 16 — 19 in the checklist are likely to be written after the first revision, but must be checked before the report is submitted. See Chapter 11 for a more detailed study of these parts of your report.

ASK A COLLEAGUE

Even if you read your report a few days after completing it and use a checklist, you may still fail to notice certain grammatical errors, information gaps and illogical deductions. This may not be because your English needs to be improved or your report writing skills need to be developed. You may have merely overlooked your grammatical errors, and since you have probably been looking at your report from one particular viewpoint your ability to evaluate the report has been affected. Therefore you need another person to consider your report with total objectivity.

Whom shall I ask?

1. Someone who will understand the subject matter.

    Since you want your report to be evaluated before you submit it, you should choose someone who has at least a basic knowledge of the subject matter. He will then be able to comment on any areas where you have provided insufficient information and perhaps guide you to new sources if necessary. He will also be able to give you feedback on your conclusions and recommendations, stating whether he finds the former logical and the latter sufficient to achieve the purpose of the report.

2. Someone who possesses good report writing skills.

    In addition to an understanding of the subject matter, this person must be someone whom you can respect as a competent report writer. You will be willing to accept criticism only from someone who has proven ability as a report writer. He will be able to comment on the use of illustrations, the adequacy of the body, the acceptability of the conclusions, and the appropriateness of the recommendations in achieving the purpose. By listening to and acting on his comments you will improve your own skills.

3. Someone who writes better English than yourself.

    If you are worried about your standard of English then you

must obtain advice from someone who is able to notice your errors and correct them. At the same time he may be able to explain to you the reasons for your errors, thus helping you to improve your English. You may write grammatically correct English, but your style may be long-winded and you may use too much jargon. He should be able to point out how you could write more concisely and clearly.

4.   Someone who will be honest with you.

The best person to give you advice is a friend who will tell you honestly what he thinks of your report without being overly critical — unless your report deserves it. Too much criticism which is to some extent unjustified is liable to depress you or make you angry with that person. Neither reaction is desirable since it can make you stubborn so that you refuse to make the improvements that are necessary. On the other hand you do not want advice from someone who refuses to criticise. You want constructive comments, not just for someone to say 'Fine', 'Well done' etc. Therefore a friend or a colleague you respect would be the most suitable choice.

After you have carried out the above three methods of revising your report and have made the necessary improvements, your report is complete and just needs some finishing touches.

11 Applying the finishing touches

Once you are satisfied that your report meets its objectives and is presented clearly and logically, you must then apply the finishing touches. The finishing touches include:

- a synopsis
- a title page
- a table of contents
- a bibliography
- a letter of transmittal

A SYNOPSIS

What is it?

As mentioned in Chapter 8, a synopsis is a summary of the purpose of the report, the main findings, the logical conclusions and the recommendations. It is sometimes called the **executive summary**, and is needed for reports that exceed about five pages. Naturally, the synopsis is written after you have made your final revision, because any major changes in the report itself will be reflected in the synopsis. If a new fact comes to light while you are writing the synopsis, you cannot just add it in there. No new information can be put in the synopsis without first including it in the body of the report.

What is its purpose?

The busy managing director may not have time to read your whole report, or he may not be sure that your report is worth reading. A synopsis enables him to ascertain the most significant aspects of your report very quickly. He can then decide whether to read the whole report.

It is apparent then that a poor synopsis of a good report is likely to lead to unjust criticism of the report. On the other hand, a poor report cannot be made good by a well written synopsis because the lack of information and the illogicality of the conclusions will still remain.

In other words a good synopsis is essential, but its quality is largely dependent on the standard of the report itself.

How do I write it?

The synopsis should be no more than 1/6th of the length of the whole report; and if the report is longer than 20 pages, the synopsis should still be limited to two or three pages.

This means that the number of paragraphs will also be limited. A rough guide to the structure of a one-page synopsis is:

Paragraph 1: Introduction
Paragraph 2 — 4: Main findings
Paragraph 5: Conclusion
Paragraph 6: Recommendations

There may, of course, be only one paragraph for the main findings of a short report; and the conclusion and recommendations may be summarised together in one paragraph. A long report, on the other hand, may require several paragraphs to summarise the main findings. The above guide must be treated with flexibility according to what is appropriate for your report.

As has been mentioned in Chapter 8, a summary requires the skilful use of linking words or connectives. Those most frequently used in the synopsis are words which indicate:

a)   additional information e.g. furthermore, moreover, not only — but also, and
b)   contrast e.g. however, on the other hand

c) result e.g. as a consequence, therefore, thus
d) purpose e.g. in order to, to

The linking words are highlighted in the executive summary below of a feasibility study report concerning the viability of setting up a joint venture company to manufacture needle bearings in the Philippines. The full report can be found in Chapter 12.

EXECUTIVE SUMMARY

The 1983 Technology Transfer Contract provided for a 10-year cooperation between Markham and Manila Bearing Factory with the option of going into a joint venture after the fourth year. Subsequently, when a Letter of Intent was signed in June 1986, both parties agreed to investigate the viability of setting up a joint venture company to manufacture needle bearings in the Philippines.

The results of this feasibility study indicate that the bearing market in the Philippines is growing steadily and should continue to do so since the Aquino government is stressing the importance of industrial expansion. However, certain segments of the market grow faster than the rest; for example, the needle bearing market has had a much higher growth rate between 1982 and 1986 compared with other types of bearings.

To supply this demand, there is a need for advanced technology and know-how to upgrade both the quality and quantity of needle bearing manufacturers in the Philippines. For the foreign partner, the joint venture strategy offers an opportunity to participate in the growth of the Philippines' bearing market. Therefore, the joint venture is a mutually beneficial endeavour in which the opportunities far outweigh the element of risk.

The joint venture would produce a number of items aimed primarily at the automotive market. Production can begin in 1989 using a new building currently belonging to the Manila Bearing Factory and equipment

Applying the finishing touches

> already imported through the technology transfer contract. Sales are projected to be $600,000 in 1989, rising to $1.95 million within five years of initial production.
>
> It is apparent, therefore, that the programme is viable, with profit after tax projected to be over 10 per cent and profit after tax return on equity averaging over 22 per cent. In addition, the joint venture should achieve foreign exchange balance and provide inflow of foreign exchange after the plant is in full operation.

A TITLE PAGE

It is important that the information given in the title page is presented clearly and attractively, since this is the first part of the report that the reader will see; a bad first impression is not always easy to change.

What goes on the title page?

1. **The title**

    The title should be fairly brief, yet precise enough for the reader to have a definite understanding of what the report is about. Consider the following pairs of titles:

    1. a) Report on Shok
        b) Impact and communication check on two Shok commercials

    2. a) The new Penang business school
        b) A feasibility study on the establishment of a business school in Penang

    In the above pairs of titles, (a) is so brief that its vagueness does not enable the reader to ascertain the precise subject of the report. In fact, 'The New Penang Business School' is misleading since it implies that the school is already in existence, whereas it is merely a feasibility study.

The (b) titles are longer, but more precise, thereby telling the reader exactly what the report is about.

2. **The author(s)**

If a report is for internal circulation only, the name of the individual author must be stated, but if it is for external use, then the name of the company will be given.

For example, the authors of the feasibility study report in Chapter 12 are 'The project team members of the Markham Company and the Manila Bearing Factory'. Here there is a group of authors who can be identified as members of the project team, and so there is no need to name them individually. It is important, though, to state that they were employees of one of the two companies concerned in the joint venture.

3. **The date**

The future reader will want to know the date of your report so that he can evaluate its relevance in terms of up-to-date information. Thus the report entitled 'Action Plan for the Property Sector' is dated February 1986, and the report on 'Shok Commercials' not only has a date of issue, but also a fieldwork date. (See Fig 11.1a)

4. **The reader's name and/or position**

This could be the name of the company for which you have written the report, or, if it is for internal use, the name of your superior.

Report on:

AN IMPACT AND COMMUNICATION CHECK OF 2 COMMERCIALS FOR SHOK CHOCOLATE DRINK

CL 7322 A

Fieldwork: September 1987

Prepared:

for: MARBELLA PTE. LTD.

by: FINE RESEARCH

November 1987

Fig. 11.1a Title page

REPORT OF THE
PROPERTY MARKET CONSULTATIVE COMMITTEE

ACTION PLAN FOR THE PROPERTY SECTOR

February 1986

Ministry of Finance
Singapore

Fig. 11.1b Title page

A TABLE OF CONTENTS

Naturally you need only write a table of contents when the report is sufficiently long to warrant one.

The table of contents enables the reader to locate the particular section of information that interests him, without having to look through the whole report to read the headings. The reader can, however, glance quickly through a short report of only a couple of pages.

A table of contents (see Figs. 4.1 and 4.2) lists the different sections and, possibly, sub-sections of your report, following the order of headings in your report. Adding the page number beside each section enables the reader to locate the relevant section without delay (See Chapter 12, Second Sample Report). In addition, this list provides the reader with an overview of the whole report, so he knows precisely what is included, and whether it contains any information appropriate to his purposes.

Similarly, a long report may require a list of figures, illustrations, tables, charts and/or a list of appendices (annexes) as shown in Figs. 11.2 and 11.3.

You must decide the amount of help your readers may require or would benefit from and then provide that assistance.

LIST OF CHARTS

	Title	Page
Chart 1	Demand and Supply of Various Types of Properties, 1980–1985	25
2	Occupancy Rates of Various Types of Properties, 1980–1985	26
3	Price Indices of Various Types of Properties, 1980–1985	27
4	Supply, Demand and Excess of Private Residential Homes by Types, September 1980–September 1985	39
5	Supply, Demand and Excess of Private Residential Homes by Geographical Area, September 1980–September 1985	40
6	Supply, Demand and Excess of Office Space by Geographical Area, September 1980–September 1985	47
7	Supply, Demand and Excess of Shop Space by Geographical Area, September 1980–September 1985	53

Fig. 11.2 List of charts
(Source: Action Plan for the Property Sector, Ministry of Finance, Singapore, 1986.)

LIST OF ANNEXES

Annex	Title	Page
1	Comparative Property Indicators of Singapore and Hong Kong	109
2	Supply and Demand of Properties, 1980–1985	111
3	Occupancy Rates of Properties, 1980–1985	112
4	Price Indices of Properties, 1980–1985	113
5	Outlook of Property Market in December 1990	114
6	Measures taken by Government/Statutory Boards to Stimulate the Economy and/or to Overcome the Property Slump, 1985	115
7	Potential Supply of Properties as of September 1983, March 1984, September 1984 and March 1985	120
8	Supply and Demand of Private Residential Homes, 1980–1985	121
9	Supply and Demand of Private Residential Homes by Locality, 1980–1985	122
10	Supply and Demand of Office Space, September 1980–September 1985	123
11	Office Rental Levels in Selected Countries, November 1985	124
12	Supply and Demand of Shop Space, September 1980–September 1985	125
13	Supply and Demand of Factory Space, November 1985	126
14	Supply and Demand of Warehouse Space, November 1985	127
15	Hotel Rooms and Visitor Arrivals, 1980–1985	128
16	Main Features of Equity Real Estate Investment Trusts in the United States	129
17	Provisions in Trust Deeds of Equity Real Estate Investment Trusts	130
18	Government Agencies and their Policy Functions in relation to the Property Sector	131
19	List of Surveys by National Development Ministry's Research and Statistics Unit and Trade and Industry Ministry's Department of Statistics	134
20	Range of Available Property Data	136
21	Private Residential Homes by Residential Status of Household Head as of June 1980	137
22	Comparative Rates and Bases of Property Tax in Selected Countries	138
23	Impact of a Reduction in Property Tax Rate on Government Revenue	139
24	Loss of Government Revenue in respect of Recommendations mainly or solely affecting the Property Sector	140
25	Members of Property Market Consultative Committee and its Sub-Committees	142
26	List of Persons seen by Property Market Consultative Committee	147

Fig. 11.3 List of annexes
(Source: Action Plan for the Property Sector, Ministry of Finance, Singapore 1986)

A BIBLIOGRAPHY

A bibliography is derived from two words:

biblios meaning 'book'
graph meaning 'write'.

Hence it is a list of books and articles that you write down at the end of your report. This list indicates your sources and will assist the reader in verifying your facts (if he wishes to do so) and in knowing where to find more information on the subject. Thus, at the end of this book there is a bibliography if you want to read more about report writing.

Note how the bibliography is written:

1. **Arrangement**

   The arrangement of the bibliography is alphabetical according to the author's surname:

   BARRASS, R. *Scientists Must Write*, Chapman and Hall, London, 1978.
   BODY, E. *Effective Written Communication*, McGraw-Hill, UK, 1979.

2. **Details of each source**

   For each source you must state

   a) author (surname and initials)
   b) title
   c) publisher
   d) place of publication
   e) date of publication
   f) edition (if necessary)

   FOWLER, H.W. *Modern English Usage*, Oxford University Press, London, 1930 (3rd edition).

   In order to distinguish clearly the author from the title, it is recommended that you use capitals, underlining or italics.

Sometimes your source is an article from a journal. In this case state the name of the author, the title of the article (in quotation marks), the name of the journal, the volume number, where appropriate, and the date.

BLAKE, T. 'Ten suggestions to start you off', *EFL Gazette*, Dec. 1982.
WILSON, D. 'Teaching students to assess their own learning', *Modern English Teacher*, 10:4, April 1983.

An alternative word to bibliography is 'references'. 'References', however, applies to sources used in your report, whereas 'bibliography' includes other books on the subject.

A LETTER OF TRANSMITTAL

After the report has been finished, it is sent under cover of a letter (or memo if the report is for someone in the same company) to the person requesting it. This letter is generally termed the letter of transmittal.

The letter of transmittal is brief. Apart from any necessary courtesies, it states the purpose and indicates that the report fulfils that purpose. The sample letter of transmittal in Fig. 11.4 is taken from the 'Report of the Property Market Consultative Committee — Action Plan for the Property Sector'. The penultimate paragraph of this letter is required only because the members of the committee feel it is necessary to reassure the Minister of Finance that they have not been 'influenced by vested interests'.

A covering memo (see Fig. 11.5) follows the same structure as the letter of transmittal.

Minister for Finance

REPORT OF THE PROPERTY MARKET CONSULTATIVE COMMITTEE - ACTION PLAN FOR THE PROPERTY SECTOR

In September 1985, you appointed us to be members of the Property Market Consultative Committee. Our terms of reference are:-

(a) to provide a regular channel for government officials and representatives of the private sector to discuss matters concerning the property market; and

(b) to draw the attention of relevant government agencies to the major problems in the property market together with our suggestions for solving those problems.

In November 1985, the First Deputy Prime Minister asked us for an action plan for the property sector.

We have completed our review. Our report is submitted herewith, together with a synopsis of our recommendations.

We see the problems in the property market as essentially threefold: unpredictable demand, excessive supply and a loss of market confidence. Our recommended solutions are accordingly addressed to these three main aspects.

We represent a wide spectrum of diverse and, sometimes, conflicting interests. To ensure that our recommendations are not influenced by vested interests, interested parties on the Committee abstained in the deliberations on matters pertaining to their organisations. For example, in Chapter 12, public sector representatives did not participate in the choice of the ministry or its components as the recommended administrative machinery to be adopted.

a

Fig 11.4 Letter of transmittal

Applying the finishing touches

We would like to take this opportunity to thank you for giving us the privilege in undertaking this review.

TOH PENG KIAT
CHAIRMAN

AU YENG KOK
MEMBER

KWEK LENG BENG
MEMBER

SONNIE LIEN
MEMBER

LIM HAN SOON
MEMBER

LIM LAN YUAN
MEMBER

LIU THAI KER
MEMBER

DAVID MA
MEMBER

NG KIM LEONG
MEMBER

PETER SEAH LIM HUAT
MEMBER

SWEE KEE SIONG
MEMBER

TAN CHOO HAW
MEMBER

TAN ENG LEONG
MEMBER

TAN WAH THONG
MEMBER

TEH KOK PENG
MEMBER

TEO TONG WAH
MEMBER

YONG KEE SENG
SECRETARY

6 FEBRUARY 1986

The Complete Asian Report Writer

> **Memorandum**
>
> To   : Mr. P. Devaraj, Personnel Officer
> From : Low Kim Cheng, Administrative Officer
> Date   : 10 February 1988
> Subject: Report on 'Absenteeism and Lack of Punctuality'
>
> The above report is submitted in accordance with your request of 18 January 1988.
>
> The report examines the extent of the problem of absenteeism and lack of punctuality. It also recommends various measures which would largely solve the problem to the satisfaction of both employees and management.

Fig 11.5 A memorandum.

12 Sample reports

The two sample reports in this chapter illustrate the key elements of a good report. They are logically organised and clearly written, so that even though the subject matter of the second report is technical, the report is readable. Readability is essential for a technical report since the readers may be more familiar with business administration than with engineering. As has been said before, your report must be written for the specific reader(s).

FIRST REPORT

On the following pages is the report that was planned in Chapter 4. Since it is fairly short, there is no need for a table of contents or a synopsis.

SIMCO PTE. LTD.

Memorandum

To : Mr. S. Raju, Divisional Manager
From : G. R. Kuek, Technical Assistant
Date : 20 March 1988
Subject: Report on 'Photography for Drawings'

The above report is being submitted in accordance with your memo dated 10 March 1988.

The report examines both the present method of obtaining photographs and an alternative method which does not require the hiring of outside photographers. It concludes that the latter system would lead to substantial savings in the long term even though it would require an initial outlay for the purchase of a suitable camera.

PHOTOGRAPHY FOR DRAWINGS

for: Mr S. Raju, Divisional Manager

G. R. Kuek
Technical Assistant
20 March 1988

PHOTOGRAPHY FOR DRAWINGS

1. INTRODUCTION

1.1 *Background*

The basic procedure for the preparation of outline or location drawings for our manuals is first to take photographs of the equipment and then to draw from them. Since the closure at the end of December 1985 of the company's photographic department we have had to use local professional photographers to take these photographs.

1.2 *Purpose*

This report examines the present system of obtaining photographs and after making a comparison with an alternative method which would require us to take our own photographs, it recommends the more efficient and economical method.

2. PRESENT METHOD

2.1 *Method of operation*

On average, the photographer visited us once a week in 1986, and took a total of 500 photographs, thus averaging about 10 photographs per week. He would then return the developed photographs to us nearly a week later. The quality of these photographs was extremely high, in fact unnecessarily high for our particular needs.

2.2 Costs

2.2.1 *Photographs*

The photographer has offered us a new contract which will cost $100 for each set of 10 photographs.

2.2.2 *Transport*

The photographer charges us $15 for each visit that he makes.

2.2.3 *Personnel*

The cost of supervising the photographer is estimated in terms of personnel time to be $20 per visit.

2.2.4 *Administration*

Administrative costs for those photographs amounted to $200 in 1986. This includes secretarial time, paperwork and postage.

2.2.5 *Total*

On the basis of the above information, annual costs for photographs can be estimated at $6,950. (See Fig 1. below)

Photographs	$100 × 50	=	5,000
Transport	$ 15 × 50	=	750
Personnel	$ 20 × 50	=	1,000
Administration			200
	Total		$ 6,950

Fig 1. Annual cost of present method

2.3 *Disadvantages*

It has become obvious that, in addition to high cost, this present system suffers from two other disadvantages.

2.3.1 *Inconvenience*

We are not able to have photographs taken at times that are always suitable for us since we have to fit in with the photographer's schedule.

2.3.2 *Speed of developing photographs*

It takes five working days for the photographs to be developed and delivered to us. Waiting a week can cause delays in the production of our manuals.

2.4 *Possible amendment*

One economy that can be made is for us to take the equipment to his studios, thereby reducing the transport cost. However, a company van is not always available when needed, and, in any case, it may not be practical to transport the equipment to his studios. Therefore this amendment to the present system is not to be recommended.

3. PROPOSED METHOD

3.1 *Method of operation*

The purchase of an instant camera would enable us to take our own photographs. These can be enlarged on our photocopier to the required size for drawings.

3.2 *Cost*

The cost of a professional quality camera with all the

necessary lenses and lights would be $2000, and it would last for 10 years. Assuming 500 photographs will be taken annually, as under the present system, the total annual cost can be estimated to be $1,975. (See Fig 2.)

Camera	$2,000 over 10 years	200
Photographs	$15 per 10 photos	750
Photocopying	5 cents p. photo	25
Personnel		1,000
	Total	$ 1,975

Fig 2. Annual cost of proposed method

Thus the proposed method would save the company $4,975 per annum.

3.3 *Advantages*

3.3.1 *Convenience*

We could take photographs at a time convenient to us, rather than according to the photographer's schedule.

3.3.2 *Speed of developing photographs*

The photographs could be developed within 24 hours if necessary and so this would cause no delays in the production of the manuals.

4. CONCLUSION

The present method of employing a photographer is proving to be excessively expensive, costing a total of $6,950 per annum for photographs which are of unnecessarily high quality. In addition, there is a delay of a week before we actually receive them.

The proposed method, on the other hand, is convenient, saves personnel time, yet still provides photographs of suitable quality. Moreover, although this system requires an initial outlay of $2,000 to purchase the camera, it would very quickly pay for itself, since over 10 years the annual costs would amount to only $1,975 per annum.

5. RECOMMENDATION

It is recommended that an instant camera be purchased to enable us to take our own photographs, thereby saving the company $4,975 per annum over 10 years.

Sample reports

SECOND REPORT

This is a feasibility study on a technical subject. The language, however, avoids the use of jargon and so the report can be easily understood by the general reader, including the chairman of the company for whom the report was written.

Please note that the figures given in the report are not to be taken as accurate, and that appendices II-IV have been omitted since they would not be of interest to readers of this book.

To   : Mr. J. Murphy, Chairman
From   : Mr. K. Y. Sim, Project Team Leader
Date   : 18 September 1987
Subject: 'Markham-Manila Joint Venture Company'

The project team members investigating the feasibility of the Markham-Manila Joint Venture Company are pleased to submit their feasibility study report as requested in your memo of 12 June 1987.

The report establishes that the joint venture would be a mutually beneficial endeavour that should be pursued since the opportunities far outweigh the element of risk involved.

BRIEF MEMO OF TRANSMITTAL

CLEAR TITLE

FEASIBILITY STUDY REPORT

FOR THE PROPOSED

MANILA-MARKHAM JOINT VENTURE
COMPANY

PREPARED JOINTLY
BY PROJECT TEAM MEMBERS

OF

THE MARKHAM COMPANY
AND THE MANILA BEARING FACTORY

September 1987

Sample reports

LOGICALLY ORGANISED AND CLEARLY SET OUT TO ENSURE QUICK LOCATION OF THE APPROPRIATE SECTIONS

Table of contents

	EXECUTIVE SUMMARY	1
I.	INTRODUCTION	3
II.	OBJECTIVES OF THE JOINT VENTURE	3
III.	THE JOINT VENTURE PARTNERS	3
	A. The Markham Company	3
	B. The Manila Bearing Factory	4
IV.	MARKET/PRODUCT CONSIDERATIONS	4
	A. Production	4
	B. Market	5
V.	OPPORTUNITIES AND RISKS	6
	A. Opportunities	6
	B. Risks	6
VI.	FINANCIAL PROJECTIONS	8
VII.	CONCLUSION	8
VIII.	RECOMMENDATION	9
	APPENDICES I — IV	10

EXECUTIVE SUMMARY

INTRODUCTION

The 1983 Technology Transfer Contract provided for a 10-year cooperation between Markham and Manila Bearing Factory with the option of going into a joint venture after the fourth year. Subsequently, when a Letter of Intent was signed in June 1986, both parties agreed to investigate the viability of setting up a joint venture company to manufacture needle bearings in the Philippines.

RESULTS OF STUDY

The results of this feasibility study indicate that the bearing market in the Philippines is growing steadily and should continue to do so since the Aquino government is stressing the importance of industrial expansion. However, certain segments of the market grow faster than the rest; for example, the needle bearing market has had a much higher growth rate between 1982 and 1986 compared with other types of bearings.

CONCLUSION — TO PROCEED WITH JOINT VENTURE

To supply this demand, there is a need for advanced technology and know-how to upgrade both the quality and quantity of needle bearing manufacturers in the Philippines. For the foreign partner, the joint venture strategy offers an opportunity to participate in the growth of the Philippines' bearing market. Therefore, the joint venture is a mutually beneficial endeavour in which the opportunities far outweigh the element of risk.

PLAN

The joint venture would produce a number of items aimed primarily at the automotive market. Production can begin in 1989 using a new building currently belonging to the Manila Bearing Factory and equipment already imported through the technology transfer contract. Sales are projected to be $600,000 in 1989, rising to $1.9 million within four years of initial production.

FINANCIAL PROJECTIONS

It is apparent, therefore, that the programme is viable, with profit after tax projected to be over 10 per cent and profit after tax return on equity averaging over 22 per

2

cent. In addition, the joint venture should achieve foreign exchange balance and provide inflow of foreign exchange after the plant is in full operation.

I. INTRODUCTION

BACKGROUND — CHRONOLOGICAL SEQUENCE

Cooperation between Markham and the Manila Bearing Factory (MBF) began in 1983 when both parties signed a Technology Transfer Contract in Manila. The contract provided for a 10-year cooperation with the option of going into joint venture after the fourth year.

PURPOSE OF THE REPORT

In June 1986, when a Letter of Intent was signed, both parties agreed to investigate the viability of setting up a joint venture company to manufacture needle bearings in the Philippines. This feasibility study report, which was jointly prepared by team members of the Markham Company and MBF, presents the results of these investigations.

II. OBJECTIVES OF THE JOINT VENTURE

THE TWO OBJECTIVES OF THE JOINT VENTURE ARE CLEARLY AND CONCISELY STATED

The primary objective of the joint venture is to become the premium supplier of needle bearings in terms of both quality and quantity in the Philippines market.

A secondary objective is to become a low-cost supplier of needle bearings in the international market.

III. THE JOINT VENTURE PARTNERS

A. The Markham Company

CLEAR NUMBERING WITH INDENTATION
I
II
III
A
B
IV

The Markham Company is the largest broad-line bearing manufacturer in the United States. Their products include needle bearings, ball bearings, tapered roller bearings, spherical roller bearings, precision components etc.

The Markham Company pioneered bearing technology in the 1930s and currently is a market leader in supplying needle bearings to the automotive industry. The company is also a major supplier of bearings in the international market, having established manufacturing plants in Australia, Argentina, France and Italy, and joint ventures in Japan, the People's Republic of China and Pakistan.

B. The Manila Bearing Factory

MBF is the premier needle bearing factory in the Philippines. Located in the capital, Manila, it employs 120 people in a factory of 8,000 square metres. It manufactures a variety of needle roller bearings and supplies primarily to the automotive market in the Philippines.

Since the signing of the Technology Transfer Contract in 1983, MBF has proved to be an extremely efficient company. Besides being cooperative, it has also shown remarkable continuity in personnel.

IV. MARKET/PRODUCT CONSIDERATIONS

A. Production

As can be seen from Fig 1, the production of bearings in the Philippines has grown steadily between 1982 and 1986, especially that of needle roller bearings. Moreover, the demand for needle bearings is projected to increase due to confidence in the new government, which is stressing the need for industrial expansion. In fact, with the anticipated upturn in the economy of the Philippines, production could reach 15 million sets by 1990.

Margin notes:

A BRIEF DESCRIPTION OF THE TWO COMPANIES WHICH EMPHASISES
i) MARKHAM'S INTERNATIONAL EXPERIENCE
ii) MBF'S SUITABILITY FOR THE JOINT VENTURE PROJECT
ONLY RELEVANT INFORMATION IS INCLUDED

THE PARAGRAPH SUMMARISES THE KEY FACT THAT EMERGES FROM THE TABLE. IT DOES NOT REPEAT ALL THE INFORMATION IN THE TABLE

The Complete Asian Report Writer

Type	1982	1983	1984	1985	1986
Needle roller bearings (millions)	4.6	5.8	7.4	8.1	9.0
Others	150	171	187	206	222
Total	154.6	176.8	194.4	214.1	231.0

Fig 1. Production of bearings in the Philippines

Production of the four types of needle roller bearings in 1986 was as follows:

Needle roller bearing type	Production in million units	%
1. Drawn Cup needle bearings	4.40	48.9
2. Solid Race needle bearings	2.00	22.2
3. U-joint bearings	1.45	16.1
4. Cage and roller assemblies	1.15	12.8
	9.00	100.0

Fig 2. Production of needle roller bearings, Philippines 1986

NOTE THE USE OF 'CONNECTIVES'

i) 'WHEREAS' TO INDICATE THAT A CONTRAST FOLLOWS

ii) 'IN OTHER WORDS' TO INTRODUCE A FURTHER EXPLANATION

B. Market

Whereas types 1 and 2 in Fig 2 are mainly for automotive applications, types 3 and 4 are for light industries, textiles, and office equipment such as typewriters and telex machines. In other words, 28.9 per cent of the needle roller bearing production was used for light industries and office equipment, and Markham is strong and experienced in serving this market.

As the economy of the Philippines expands over

the next few years, so there will be a wider market for all types of needle roller bearing, but especially types 3 and 4 (Drawn Cup and Solid Race needle bearings).

V. OPPORTUNITIES AND RISKS

   A. **Opportunities**

   The opportunities presented by pursuing a joint venture strategy with MBF include the following:

   (i) active participation in a growth market;
   (ii) active participation in a product in which Markham is strong and enjoys a reputation for quality;
   (iii) tie-up with a top Philippine needle bearing manufacturer;
   (iv) the existence of a group of customers in Philippine-foreign automotive joint ventures who consider the Manila-Markham Company the logical choice for local sourcing;
   (v) the possible source of a low-cost supplier for the long-term Markham worldwide supply strategy; and
   (vi) powerful leverage to ensure Markham's place as a world-class player in the bearing business in the years to come.

   > THE LISTING OF THE VARIOUS OPPORTUNITIES ENABLES THE READER TO UNDERSTAND THESE OPPORTUNITIES WITH SPEED AND CLARITY

   B. **Risks**

   As with other bold steps in business, joint venturing in the Philippines is not without risks.

   i) Competition

   German and Japanese competitors are already involved in the bearing market in the Philippines. The former, GDS, has already

   > WELL PLANNED SO THAT EACH RISK HAS A SEPARATE SUB-HEADING

signed know-how and technical agreements with several Manila-based companies. The Japanese competitor, Niki, has been providing training for 90 Filipino engineers and technicians since 1985. As these trainees return to the Philippines, they are engaged by top local companies and hold key positions. Naturally, they promote Japanese products.

ii) Political instability

> **NOTE THE USE OF SHORT SENTENCES SO THAT EACH SENTENCE CONTAINS ONE POINT**
>
> **THE 'CONNECTIVES' SHOW THE LINK BETWEEN SENTENCES E.G. IN ADDITION, IN OTHER WORDS**
>
> **'HOWEVER' INTRODUCES A CONTRAST WITH THE BAD NEWS**
>
> **'THEREFORE' INTRODUCES THE LOGICAL CONCLUSION**

Since February 1986, when the Marcos government was overthrown by 'people power' and Cory Aquino became president, there have been three coup attempts. The most recent one, which took place in August 1987, drew its support from a section of the military where there is still a certain amount of dissatisfaction. In addition, the communist New People's Army (NPA) is posing a considerable threat in the provinces to the authority of Mrs. Aquino's government. In other words, there is no assurance of political stability in the Philippines, and a new government would be almost certain to have an adverse effect on a joint venture project. However, there is growing confidence in the government boosted by an upturn in the economy.

The risk posed by political instability may indicate that it would be prudent to adopt a 'wait and see' strategy. However, such a strategy would merely enable our competitors to corner the market. With that in mind, the real risk to our company is, therefore, how much it would cost us if we did not proceed with this joint venture project.

VI. FINANCIAL PROJECTIONS

Since the financial projections form the most essential part of this report, all assumptions or key operating conditions were discussed and agreed upon by both parties.

Sales are projected to rise steadily to $1.95 million in 1993 from $600,000 in 1989. The graph in Appendix I shows the sales projections from 1989-1993.

<small>THE MAIN FACT IS NOTED HERE, WITH REFERENCE TO THE DETAILS IN AN APPENDIX</small>

Other financial projections, such as the proforma income statement, balance sheet, and the foreign exchange balance statement can be found in Appendices II-IV.

<small>DETAILS ARE IN THE APPENDICES</small>

These projections indicate that total registered capital is planned at $3 million, and each partner will contribute 50 per cent in a combination of cash, equipment and technology.

Labour costs in the Philippines are still relatively low, even though employees in a joint venture project involving a foreign company would receive a considerably higher wage than those in local enterprises. We have projected a total cost of $300 per employee per month, including benefits, for the joint venture.

Based on these projections, profit after tax is estimated to be over 10 per cent and profit after tax return on equity will average over 22 per cent. In addition, the joint venture should achieve foreign exchange balance after the plant is in full operation.

VII. CONCLUSION

There is a certain amount of risk involved in proceeding with this joint venture, since there is competition and the Philippines cannot guarantee political stability.

<small>SUMMARY OF THE MAIN POINTS:

RISKS INVOLVED</small>

OPPORTUNITY

PROJECTED DEMAND, SALES AND PROFIT

THE BAD NEWS IS AT THE BEGINNING AND SO THE GOOD NEWS AT THE END POINT THE WAY TO THE RECOMMENDATION

GO AHEAD!

9

However, this tie-up with a top Philippine needle bearing manufacturer is an excellent opportunity to establish Markham as one of the leading bearing companies in the world for the next decade.

The demand for bearings is growing steadily in the Philippines and it is projected that sales from the joint venture would be $600,000 in 1989 rising to $1.95 million in 1993. This is estimated to lead to a profit after tax of over 10 per cent and to an average profit after tax return on equity of over 22 per cent.

VIII. RECOMMENDATION

Since this feasibility study points to a viable programme, with the potential benefits far outweighing the element of risk, it is recommended that the joint venture company should be established without delay.

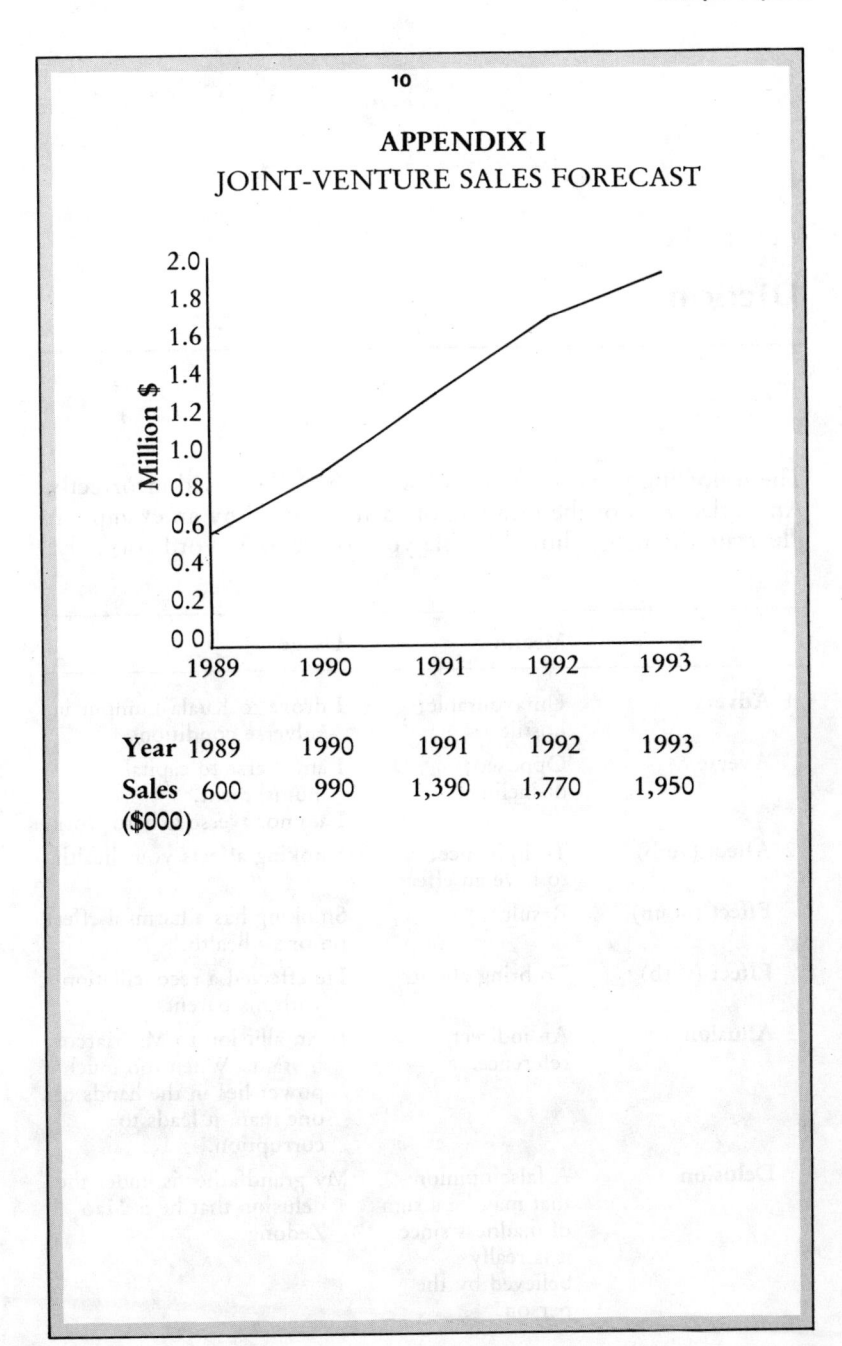

APPENDIX I
JOINT-VENTURE SALES FORECAST

Year	1989	1990	1991	1992	1993
Sales ($000)	600	990	1,390	1,770	1,950

APPENDIX 1

Diction

The following pairs or groups of words are often used incorrectly. An explanation of the meaning of each followed by an example to illustrate the usage should enable you to use each word correctly.

	Meaning	Usage
1 **Adverse**	Unfavourable; hostile.	I drove to Kuala Lumpur in adverse conditions.
Averse	Opposed; disinclined.	I am averse *to* capital punishment. I am not averse *to* hard work.
2 **Affect** (verb)	To influence; to have an effect.	Smoking affects your health.
Effect (noun)	Result.	Smoking has a harmful effect on one's health.
Effect (verb)	To bring about.	He effected a reconciliation with his parents.
3 **Allusion**	An indirect reference.	In an allusion to Mr Marcos, he said, 'When too much power lies in the hands of one man, it leads to corruption.'
Delusion	A false opinion that may be a sign of madness since it is really believed by the person.	My grandfather is under the delusion that he is Mao Zedong.

Appendix 1: Diction

	Meaning	Usage
Illusion	The seeing of something that does not exist. A false impression.	I was under the illusion that the goods were going to be delivered yesterday. (This is a strong criticism of the reader's company.)
4 Assure	To say with certainty; to promise.	I assure you that this error will not occur again.
Assurance	a. Belief in one's ability.	He lacks assurance.
	b. Promise.	I give you my assurance that this will not happen again.
	c. Insurance against death.	Do you have a life assurance policy?
Insure	To protect oneself against loss by *insurance*.	The factory is not adequately insured against fire.
Ensure	To make sure.	Please ensure that we receive the goods by the end of October.
5 Contagious	That can be spread by touch (disease).	Do you think AIDS is contagious?
Infectious	That can be spread by germs usually in the air (disease)	Colds are very infectious.
Contagious/ Infectious	That can be spread (figuratively).	His laughter is contagious/ infectious.
6 Council	A group of people appointed to make decisions, rules, etc.	The town council decided to construct a new recreation centre.
Councillor	A member of a council.	
Counsel	Advice.	The counsellor gave the students excellent advice.
Counsellor	An adviser.	
7 Disinterested	Impartial.	The Cup Final referee was totally disinterested.
Uninterested	Not interested.	My wife is uninterested in football.

187

	Meaning	Usage
8 Imply	To suggest.	Are you implying that I am lying?
Infer	To deduce (a speaker or writer implies, a listener or reader infers).	The workers inferred that the company would have to retrench some staff.
9 Increase	Rise.	There has been a steady increase in property prices this year.
Increment	Rise in money, especially salary.	In our company we receive two increments a year.
10 Inflammable/ Flammable	Able to be set on fire easily.	Keep your distance, that lorry is carrying a flammable liquid.
Non-flammable	Cannot be set on fire easily.	Children's clothes should always be non-flammable.
11 Judicial	Related to a court of law or a judge.	We shall have to take judicial proceedings against you.
Judicious	Having sound judgement.	The board made a judicious decision.
12 Practicable	Feasible, can be done. (Cannot be used with reference to people.)	This plan seems practicable.
Practical	Concerned with action; can be done and is useful.	Your invention will be extremely practical.
	(People) Clever at doing things and dealing with difficulties.	He is always making improvements to our flat; such a practical person.
13 Principal	(adj.) Main, most important. (noun) Head (of schools).	My principal concern is to see this company through the recession.
Principle	General truth, rule.	I believe in the principle of freedom of speech.

Appendix 1: Diction

	Meaning	Usage
In principle	In general	They agreed to the plan in principle, but there were several details they did not like.
14 **Raise** (verb)	To lift, *collect together*, bring up a family, *make higher*.	We need to raise sufficient capital to overcome the present crisis. He raised the rent.
Rise (verb)	To come up, go up, increase.	Prices have risen a lot recently.
Raise/Rise (noun)	An increase in pay.	He received a raise. (American) He received a rise. (British)
15 **Seating**	Provision or arranging of seats.	What is the seating capacity of the room? She arranged the seating for the lecture.
Sitting	A period of time spent sitting in a chair; a meeting of an official body.	He read the book at one sitting. The committee were expecting a long sitting.

189

APPENDIX 2
Spelling

Some people find no difficulty with English spelling, whereas others never quite manage to master its complexities. In his book *Origin of the Alphabet*, Joseph Naveh writes:

'But as bad as English spelling may be, it still retains most of the principles of alphabetic writing. It takes only a year or two of study to learn to spell English. The Chinese, on the other hand, have to devote many years to learning characters if they are to have a complete command of their literature.'

Your spelling of English will improve if you observe a few rules and make an effort to learn the correct spelling of those words which cause particular difficulty.

GENERAL RULES

1 When 's' is added to words ending in 'y', the ending becomes '-ies'.

carry + s = carries
company + s = companies

But when the letter before the 'y' is a vowel, the ending becomes '-ys'.

play + s = plays
key + s = keys

2 When a suffix (the letters added to the end of a word) beginning with a vowel (e.g. '-ing', '-er') is added to a word of one

syllable of which the last two letters are one vowel and finally one consonant, that consonant must be doubled.

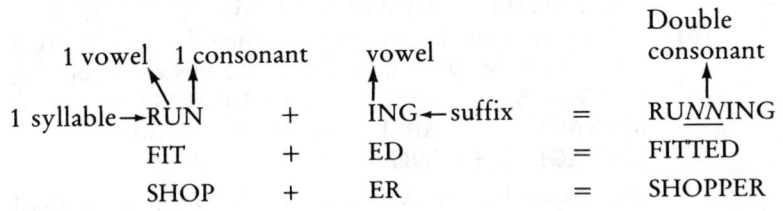

```
                                              Double
   1 vowel  1 consonant      vowel            consonant
1 syllable→RUN      +     ING←suffix    =     RUNNING
           FIT      +     ED            =     FITTED
           SHOP     +     ER            =     SHOPPER
```

3   Rule 2 applies also to words of two syllables when the stress is on the second syllable.

```
BEGIN    +   ING  =  BEGINNING
                     stress on second syllable,
                     so double 'N'

ANSWER   +   ED   =  ANSWERED
                     stress on first syllable,
                     so single 'R'
```

This rule explains the spelling of the following words:

refer	referred	reference
	↑ stress	↑ stress
occur	occurred	occurrence
prefer	preferred	preference
market	marketed	marketing
credit	credited	creditor
benefit	benefited	benefiting

4   Where a word ends in a single 'e', this 'e' is omitted when a suffix beginning with a vowel is added.

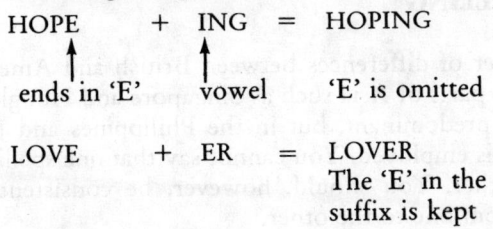

```
       HOPE    +   ING   =   HOPING
        ↑           ↑
   ends in 'E'    vowel      'E' is omitted

       LOVE    +   ER    =   LOVER
                             The 'E' in the
                             suffix is kept
```

191

BUT (a) if the word ends in double 'e', both are kept before the suffix '-ing'.
GUARANTEE   GUARANTEEING
(b) if the word ends in '-ce' or '-ge', then the 'e' is omitted only when the suffix begins with the vowels 'e' or 'i'.
COURAGE + OUS   = COURAGEOUS
MANAGE   + ABLE = MANAGEABLE
MANAGE   + ING   = MANAGING

The reason for this is that when a 'c' or 'g' is followed by an 'a', 'o' or 'u' it is pronounced with a hard 'c' (like a 'k') and 'g':

e.g. cat, go

When 'c' and 'g' are followed by 'e' or 'i' they are usually soft:

e.g. cinema, gentle

Thus, in order for 'courage' and 'manage' to be pronounced with a soft 'g', the 'e' must be kept when the suffix begins with 'a', 'o', or 'u':

COURAGEOUS, MANAGEABLE

The soft pronunciation of 'c' and 'g' before 'i' means that the 'e' can be omitted in MANAGING without affecting the pronunciation of the 'g'.

5   To choose between 'ie' and 'ei' when the sound is 'ee', 'i comes before e except after c' is a good rule:

e.g.   bel*ie*ve, n*ie*ce, ch*ie*f
but, after c,   rece*i*pt, ce*i*ling, dece*i*ve.

This rule applies only when the sound of the 'ie' or 'ei' is 'ee'. The exceptions to this rule are:

counterfeit, seize, weird

AMERICAN SPELLING

There are a number of differences between British and American spelling. In certain parts of Asia such as Singapore and Hongkong, British spelling is predominant, but in the Philippines and Japan American spelling is employed. You cannot say that one spelling is better than the other. You should, however, be consistent and avoid switching from one to the other.

Appendix 2: Spelling

	American	British
1	**-or** favorite labor color	**-our** favourite labour colour
2	**-er** center fiber theater	**-re** centre fibre theatre
3	**-og** catalog dialog	**-ogue** catalogue dialogue
4	**-ense** defense offense license	**-ence (noun)** defence offence licence (verb: license)
5	**-ize** **-yze** realize analyze	**-ise or -ize** **-yse** realise or realize analyse
6	final **-l** when unstressed traveler traveled leveled	**-ll** traveller travelled levelled

Individual Words

American	British
aluminum	aluminium
check (from a bank)	cheque
fulfillment	fulfilment
jewelry	jewellery
pajamas	pyjamas
plow	plough
program	programme
specialty	speciality
sulfur	sulphur
tire	tyre

COMMON ASIAN PROBLEM WORDS

absence	embarrass	originate
acceptable	exaggerate	parallel
accessories	except	pronunciation
accommodation	explanation	receipt
accompanying	extension	recipient
accustomed	extraordinary	referred
achievement	feasible	regrettable
acknowledge	financial	representative
address	foreign	rhythm
adjust	forfeit	scarcity
all right	forty	schedule
apologise (verb)	government	secretary
apology/ies (noun)	guarantee	separate
appreciate	humorous	similar
argument	immediately	subsidiary
authorize	independent	substitute
auxiliary	initiative	successful
beneficial	installation	supplementary
benefit	irrelevant	systematic
business	laboratory	technician
calendar	liable	technique
commission	maintain	temporarily
committee	maintenance	tendency
competitive	manufacture	thoroughly
concede	merchandise	unanimous
conscientious	miscellaneous	until
convenience	necessary	vacancy
definite	negligence	variety
deficit	noticeable	versatile
depreciation	obsolete	warehouse
description	occasionally	warranty
development	official	yield

APPENDIX 3

Grammar

It is not possible in a brief appendix to give a comprehensive analysis of English grammar. There are, however, certain grammatical errors which are frequently made by Asians and I shall focus on these.

Plurals

The following words must *not* be used in the plural. In other words, do not put an 's' at the end of the word.

accommodation (accommodations exists, however, in American English)	cutlery
	equipment
	furniture
	information
advice	luggage/baggage
clothing	machinery
crockery	traffic

Since there is no plural, when you write about a quantity you must use **some**, or **any** in questions and negatives.

> I need **some** advice.
> Do you require **any** new machinery?
> We do not have **any** equipment.

Since there is no plural, these words are uncountable. In other words, you cannot have 'one advice' or 'an advice', etc. If you want to use 'one' with reference to the above words, you must say

> a piece of advice
> an item of furniture
> an article of clothing
> a piece of equipment

Subject/Verb Agreement

Mistakes are often made with regard to subject/verb agreement. If the subject is singular, then the verb is singular:

> The production manager assures me that ...

If the subject is plural, then the verb is plural:

> Certain exceptional circumstances prevent us from ...

Difficulties arise when:

(a) the subject is a long way from the verb.

> *Absenteeism* among the factory workers who live in outlying districts *has* increased 20 per cent since the last survey.

(b) expressions such as 'together with', 'as well as' and 'including' are used.

These expressions do not affect the number (singular or plural form) of the verb:

> The chief accountant, as well as her two assistants, has examined the company accounts.
> The consignment, including the additional order, was shipped according to schedule.

(c) the words 'each', 'every', 'everybody', 'anybody' are used. These words take the singular form of the verb:

> Every employee is entitled to a 15-minute tea break.

(d) collective or group nouns are used e.g. staff, committee, company, public, audience.

It is possible to use either the singular or the plural:

The staff **is/are** going to receive one month's bonus.
The committee **has/have** decided to approve the proposal.

However, when the group is being thought of as a whole undivided unit, it is better to use the singular.

The company **is** opening an office in Bangkok.

The plural should be used when the individual parts of the group are being considered.

The executive staff **are** listed on page 28 of the annual report.

In general, when there is no particular emphasis on either the whole or the parts of the group noun, there is greater use of the plural in British English than in American English. This means that whether you use the singular or the plural, you will be correct.

Will and Would

Will is used to refer to something that is going to happen in the future, either as a prediction or an intention.

The expansion of the factory premises will lead to increased profits.
The project team will inspect the recently laid pipeline.

Would is used:

(a) in reported speech instead of 'will'.

At a meeting with the company supervisors it was agreed that they would monitor the situation carefully.

(b) with the words 'like' and 'appreciate'.

The workers would like to discuss incentives with management.

It would be appreciated if management could ...

Both **will** and **would** are used when there is a **condition** which is either stated or implied.

Improvements in the public transportation system will/would reduce the problem of lack of punctuality.

The implied condition is 'If implemented'. If the condition is likely to be fulfilled, i.e. if there are likely to be improvements, then use 'will'.

'(If they are implemented) improvements in the public transportation system will reduce the problem of lack of punctuality.'

However, if the condition is not likely to be fulfilled, use 'would'.

'(If they were implemented) improvements in the public transportation system would reduce the problem of lack of punctuality.'

Subjunctive

Recommendations are frequently written in the subjunctive.

It is recommended that the situation be monitored carefully over the next six months.

The form of the subjunctive is usually the base form of the verb, or the infinitive without the 'to'.

It is recommended that the committee *approve* the proposal to expand the factory premises.

Appendix 3: Grammar

The only exception to this rule is the verb 'be' which has a past form 'were' in addition to the present subjunctive 'be'.

If I *were* you ...

The subjunctive is commonly used in reports with the following words:

(a) the verbs 'recommend', 'propose', 'suggest', 'order', 'command', 'insist'.

> The Singapore government has suggested that every graduate mother *have* three children.

(b) the adjectives 'vital', 'essential', 'important', 'desirable', 'advisable', when they are used with 'it is'.

> *It is vital* that every child *receive* a sound education.

In British English, the word 'should' is frequently added, thus avoiding the subjunctive.

> The Singapore government has suggested that every graduate mother *should* have three children.

Infinitive or Participle

Report writers frequently have to choose between the infinitive and the participle (-ing).

The watchman did not remember { to switch on the alarm. / switching on the alarm

not remember + INFINITIVE = forget
not remember + -ING = not recall

In the above sentence, the more likely meaning is that he forgot i.e. he did not remember *to switch* on the alarm.

A good grammar book will provide you with detailed lists but the most common problem occurs when the preposition 'to' is used.

> The workers are used *to* receiv*ing* an annual bonus equivalent to one month's salary.

The expression is [used to] + [-ing].
In other words, 'to' goes with 'used' and so the form of the verb that follows is not the infinitive.
Similarly:

> Accustomed to
> Look forward to
> With a view to
> Contribute to

> e.g. I look forward to hear*ing* from you.
> The expansion of the factory contributed a great deal *to ensuring* higher profits.

APPENDIX 4

Punctuation

The purpose of punctuation is to make your meaning clear, and this is easier to achieve by means of short sentences. However, unless attention is paid to the use of commas within sentences there may still be some ambiguity.

Use of commas

- The apprentice watched the supervisor carefully taking down notes.

What did the apprentice do carefully? Did he watch the supervisor carefully, or did he take down notes carefully?

The comma generally represents a pause in spoken English, and so it indicates how phrases are grouped. Thus, each of the two meanings can be clarified by the addition of a comma in the appropriate place.

> The apprentice watched the supervisor carefully, taking down notes.

or

> The apprentice watched the supervisor, carefully taking down notes.

- The boss left the workers feeling very depressed.

Who was depressed, the boss or the workers? Without the comma it is the workers who were feeling depressed. If the boss were feeling depressed, the sentence should be:

The boss left the workers, feeling very depressed.

Commas with relative clauses

What is the difference in meaning between the following sentences:

1. Dogs which bark should be shot.
2. Dogs, which bark, should be shot.

Sentence 1 contains an identifying or restrictive relative clause. In other words, it consists of *one* idea and the relative clause 'which barks' merely identifies which dogs should be shot.

Sentence 2, however, contains a non-restrictive relative clause, and this means that *two* statements are being made about dogs:

a. Dogs bark.
b. Dogs should be shot. (All of them!)

Since there are two statements being made, the commas are required.

Here is another example:

Fighter pilots, who lack skill and nerve, never survive long.

With the commas, there are two statements about fighter pilots:

a. They lack skill and nerve.
b. They never survive long.

This is, of course, not the intended meaning. Removal of the commas makes 'who lack skill and nerve' a restrictive or identifying relative clause, and so it means 'those fighter pilots who lack skill and nerve never survive long'.

Too many commas

The comma should be used to aid quick and unambiguous understanding of the sentence. Nevertheless you should take care not to over-use commas for this will make your reports very jerky to read.

The opening sentence of the executive summary on Page 176 could be punctuated as follows:

> The 1983 Technology Transfer Contract provided for a ten-year cooperation, between Markham and Manila Bearing Factory, with the option of going into a joint venture, after the fourth year.

The original version flows more smoothly because there are no commas:

> The 1983 Technology Transfer Contract provided for a ten-year cooperation between Markham and Manila Bearing Factory with the option of going into a joint venture after the fourth year.

Bibliography

BARRASS, R., *Scientists Must Write*, Chapman and Hall, London, 1978.
BODY, E., *Effective Written Communication*, McGraw-Hill, UK, 1979.
COMFORT, J., REVELL, R., and STOTT, C., *Business Reports in English*, Cambridge University Press, 1984.
COOPER, B.M., *Writing Technical Reports*, Penguin Books, Middlesex, 1964.
FOWLER, H.W., *Modern English Usage*, Oxford University Press, London, 1930, (3rd edition).
GOWERS, SIR ERNEST, *The Complete Plain Words*, H.M.S.O., London, 1954.
GRAVES, H.P., and HOFFMAN, L.S., *Report Writing*, Prentice-Hall Inc., New Jersey, 1974, (4th edition).
IACONE, S.J., *Modern Business Report Writing*, MacMillan, 1985.
JOSEPH, A., *Put It in Writing*, Deltak, U.S.A., 1985.
MOORE, N., and HESP, M., *The Basics of Writing Reports Etcetera*, Clive Bingley Ltd., London, 1985.
PAULEY, S., *Technical Report Writing Today*, Houghton Miflin, Boston, 1973.
Report of the Committee on Productivity in the Manufacturing Sector (1985), National Productivity Board, Singapore, 1986.
SWANSEN, S., *For Your Information: A Guide to Writing Reports*, Prentice-Hall Inc., New Jersey, 1965.
What Else Can We Learn from the Japanese?, National Productivity Board, Singapore, undated.

Bibliography

WOOLCOTT, L.A., and UNWIN, W.R., *Mastering Business Communication*, MacMillan, 1983.

Index

Abbreviations 80
Accuracy 4, 43, 142, 146
Ambiguity 84-88, 99, 144-145
Appendices 55-57, 118-119, 146, 157-159, 183, 185

Background 16, 39, 60-61, 63, 65, 67, 68, 141, 168, 178
Bibliography 147, 160-161

Checklist 141-147
Conclusion 56, 145
   definition of 122-123
   examples of 127-128, 171-172, 183-184
   where to put 124-126

Definition of terms 61-62
Diagrams 117-118

Flow charts 117-119
Form reports 5-8

Glossary 80
Grammar 74, 99, 144, 148-149, 191-196
Graphs 106-109, 112-113, 143

Headings 29, 44-48, 51-55, 68, 103, 181
   examples of 46-47
Histograms 115

Ideas 3, 89
Illustrations 102, 143
   purpose of 104-106

   types of 110-117
   where to put 118-119
Information 2, 8
   ordering of 48-49, 142
   organisation of 47-48, 142
   recording 29
   selection of 40-44, 51
   sources of 20-22, 146
Interviews 22
   conducting 24-25
   preparing for 22-24
Introduction 38
   examples of 63-67, 168, 176, 178
   purpose of 58
   scope of 59

Language 4, 70, 133
   clarity of 4, 78, 82, 99, 132, 144, 181
   cohesiveness of 88, 99
   collocation 73
   completeness of 4
   conciseness of 4, 45, 74, 77, 99, 132, 144
   connotation 71-73
   correctness of 70, 98
   denotation 71
   diction 70, 95, 144
   jargon 17, 79-80
   linking words 90-92, 151-153
   punctuation 74, 133-135, 137, 138, 144
   repetition 74-75
   spelling 73
   tautology 75
   transition sentences 45, 78